KT-364-766

INSPIRED BY A BLANK SCREEN

RE-BOOT YOUR SPIRITUAL LIFE

Irene Howat

CHRISTIAN
FOCUS

Irene Howat is an award-winning author who is accomplished writer in writing for children and adults. She has many titles to her name, including *My Beloved Russia*(ISBN 978-1-84550-062-7) and *A Week in the Life of MAF*(ISBN 978-1-84550-940-9). She is married to a minister and they have a grown up family. She is also a talented artist and lives in Argyll, Scotland.

Unless otherwise indicated Scripture quotations are taken from the *Holy Bible, New International Version*. Copyright © 1973, 1978, 1984 by International Bible Society. Used by permission of Hodder & Stoughton Publishers, A member of the Hodder Headline Group. All rights reserved. NIV is a registered trademark of the International Bible Society. UK trademark number 1448790.

© Christian Focus Publications 2007

ISBN 1-84550-263-9
ISBN 978-1-84550-263-8

10 9 8 7 6 5 4 3 2 1

Published in 2007
by
Christian Focus Publications Ltd,
Geanies House, Fearn, Ross–shire
IV20 1TW, Scotland

www.christianfocus.com

Cover design by moose77.com

Printed by Nørhaven Paperback A/S, Denmark

All rights reserved. No part of this publication may be reproduced, stored in a retrieval system, or transmitted in any form or by any means, electronic, mechanical, photocopying, recording or otherwise, without the prior permission of the publisher or a license permitting restricted copying. In the U.K. such licenses are issued by the Copyright Licensing Agency, 90 Tottenham Court Road, London W1P 9HE.

INSPIRED
BY A
BLANK SCREEN

For
my fellow members of the
Scottish Fellowship of Christian Writers

CONTENTS

FOREWORD

BY

HELEN ROSEVEARE

A fascinating idea - that by familiarising myself with the workings of a word-processor document on my computer, I can understand better how to live the Christian life!

From the first comment, 'the intimidation of the **blank screen**', I felt at home. When I obtained my first computer, over twenty years ago, I called it my Beast - it intimidated and terrified me. Without doubt, 'it' was the Boss, and I was its slave. An hour's tutorial with a kindly friend assured me, that if I called 'it' my Friend, I would gain a psychological victory! That was my start.

Likewise, to live the Christian life may seem a frightening impossibility to a new beginner, until the assurance is given that God is our Friend, and freely gives us His Spirit to guide and direct us through all the difficulties and problems of life.

I loved the chapter on learning to **file** everything - what a blessing to learn how to tidy up the mess of one's study, and equally of one's Christian life: and how to **delete** what doesn't need filing - holding no grudges, forgiving and forgetting, whatever occurs that is not pleasing to our

Lord. Then **saving** and **printing** all that is of value - how easy to forget, and then there is a power cut and all the day's work is lost! Is it not the same spiritually - that all He teaches us day by day be saved in our hearts and printed out in our daily lives. **Copy** and **paste** has been the life blood of thousands of us writers, saving endless hours of re-typing and re-arranging - and should provide us with a clear picture as we think of our need to 'be holy as He is', imitating our Lord and Saviour, being humble and meek, obedient and compassionate as Jesus.

Then the **ruler** and **toolbar** to guide us into making the fullest possible use of all the program's facilities, so as to produce work of the highest possible excellence - living by the Ten Commandments, and understanding them as rules to help us imitate Him. I confess the **help** button has often left me more puzzled than before - as Irene says 'swimming through mud!' - but how wonderful to know there is always the Helper on hand for our spiritual needs, when we acknowledge our need of Him.

Shut-down at the end of a hard day's work is a marvellous moment, and so we can each trust that our own passing on from this life into the nearer presence of our Lord will be a good 'shut-down - a falling asleep in Jesus. Yes, and the final chapter on **Restart** - how thrilling to start again, the next chapter in our eternal life in the presence of the Master, 'the eternal joys of heaven'!

Over the course of twenty years, I have learned to use my word-processor fairly efficiently: as I read this book, I felt deeply challenged as to whether I had learned equally thoroughly how to live the Christian life - not merely efficiently, but more importantly, as a humble 'copy' of the life of my Lord and Saviour.

Helen Roseveare

1

INTIMIDATED OR INSPIRED?

Every writer knows the feeling, whether they write long books or short letters, whether they write thank-you notes for Christmas presents or complaints when a product fails to live up to expectations. And the feeling? Intimidation. It's brought on by a blank sheet of paper or a blank computer screen. Our minds go as blank as the paper and screen. What do we want to say? How do we want to say it? Where do we begin? How often I've been there!

It was not always so. I remember when, as a child, I was given a new exercise book at school. A new book always seemed so clean, white and fresh compared to the dog-eared one it replaced. Resolving to write more neatly, to draw more carefully and to make fewer mistakes, I would launch into the pristine blankness of page one. The first couple of sheets were often models of what was possible. But before long the writing deteriorated, the page corners began to curl and the teacher's red corrections discouraged me. By the time I reached the staples that marked the middle of the book it had become just like every previous one. Perhaps that experience repeated book upon book, year upon year, was what changed a blank sheet of paper from being a treat to being a challenge ... to being plain intimidating. And a blank computer screen is just an electronic version of the same.

I love writing books; it must be one of the best jobs in the world. Being a biographer allows me to spend as long as I need researching someone of interest before committing a single word to a page. All those about whom I've written have been Christians and researching their lives is often a great blessing, so much so that there is sometimes a very fine line between work and recreational reading, in the real meaning of re-creational. I search out sources from all sorts of places, read book after book and spend hours on line. Before a word is written down I need to feel that I am the person about whom I'm writing. And a trick from my childhood helps me to do that.

When I was a little girl I had my very own supersonic mode of travel, and that was some time before Concorde first zipped through the skies. It was my tick-boat. For years my tick-boat was my secret; I told nobody about it, even my nearest and dearest. I guess I thought that they would have laughed at me. They would! But over the last few years I've been asked by many people how to develop their writing skills, and it seems to me that a tick-boat is an invaluable tool. So, at the risk of being laughed at, I'll unveil my childhood's nocturnal transportation.

At night, when I went to bed, I decided where I wanted to go to and who I wanted to be. The place could be anywhere in the world, or beyond – for this was in the days when space travel was the stuff of my brothers' weekly comics. And the person could be anyone at all, past, present or future. As my favourite book was *The Girl's Book of Heroines*, I often chose to be one of its characters. So, with the light out and my eyes tightly closed, I imagined I was in a tick-boat. I've no idea what it was meant to look like, but it derived its name from the 'fact' that it could transport me to wherever I wanted to be in a single tick of the bedroom clock.

Come with me on one such journey. Just one tick from reality I was in the Crimea, walking through a hospital hut with Florence Nightingale. I would hold out my hands – quite literally – and imagine that I could feel the rough blankets that covered the soldiers and the warmth of their fevered foreheads. Then I went through my other senses, trying to smell the combination of heat, illness and boiling cabbage; to listen to wounded soldiers moaning, men snoring, Florence Nightingale ordering nurses around and comforting her patients, and all against the distant sound of war; to taste the food they ate and feel the dust of the Crimea in my mouth. And I would 'look' all around myself taking in the tiniest details that my childish imagination conjured up as the Crimean War.

That was all a long time ago. Yet now, when I'm writing biography, I do exactly the same. Having discovered as much as I can about my subject, I use my old tick-boat technique and try to feel, smell, hear, taste and see what he or she experienced. When I was writing one book I phoned the subject twelve week-nights in succession, reading a chapter of the book to her each night. At the end of nearly every call she said, 'That's right, but how did you know? I didn't tell you.' And my answer was that when I was writing the material I felt as though I *was* her and could imagine her feelings and reactions even though she hadn't discussed them with me.

This brings me right back to the beginning. Why is it that however much research has been done, however much I 'am' the subject, I'm still intimidated by the blank computer screen? It still bullies me into inactivity. It was on one such occasion that I spent some time looking at the screen for inspiration ... and realised it wasn't blank at all! All sorts of prompts were trying to give me a kick-start. And, when I scrolled down the prompts on the various tool bars I realised that the 'blank' computer screen was providing me with inspiration, not for the book I was working on, but for this one!

Computers are nothing if they are not well organised. My earliest encounter with a computer was a programming class I attended in the days when the computer took up a whole room in our local college. Probably the only thing of lasting worth I remember was that computers behave logically and that to make the most of them we have to try to think in a straight line. That is no criticism of the course I attended, rather a tribute to the speed with which technology has moved on. Users of computers no longer need to understand how they work! In fact, I have found it a helpful exercise to use my computer prompts – its blank screen – to examine how I work, how I think and, from time to time, what I believe.

2

FILE

It seems to me that there are two kinds of people in the world; there are filers and there are pilers. Filers can lay their hands on anything from an ancient recipe to the dog's vaccination card in less time than it takes to ask for it. Pilers know where it is but can't understand why it's not there. Both groups have a motto. The filers' motto is 'Just a minute and I'll get it for you.' And the pilers' motto is 'I don't understand it. It *was* there.' Are there life-lessons to be learned from filers and pilers and the computer's insistence that we file everything? I think there are, and I say that as a congenital piler who has had to become a filer to survive.

Welcome to my study. It's about twelve feet by nine feet and is a small room in our home. It takes me about thirty seconds to walk to work, and that's taking it slowly! When we first moved to our present home my study was also a spare bedroom, theoretically. Thankfully, as the daughter whose bedroom it was had the good sense to get married and take her things to her own home, I was soon able to dispense with the single bed that seemed to take up most of the space. However, until it departed I used it as my filing cabinet. Some people have suspension files, others have drawer files … and I had my very own bed file. The idea was not original; it was one of the many things I learned from reading Francis Schaeffer! The bed was covered by a sheet of chipboard, and the chipboard was covered with piles and piles of paper. At that time I did as much editing as writing and it was my recurring fear that I'd get manuscripts mixed up! A regular dream was that I was drowning in paper. Whatever happened to the paperless office we were promised two decades ago?

I suppose it was that organised chaos that inspired me to spend some time thinking how to arrange the room when the bed was removed. The one thing necessary was that I should know where things are. Like the grandmother who embroidered names on the sweaters she knitted for her identical twin two-year-old grandsons, I realised that the easiest way to identify things is to name them – boldly! Like so many of life's little discoveries it's not rocket science, but it certainly changed my study! In the old bed-file days finding a specific sheet of paper could sometimes be like searching for a particular bluebell in a wood; now at least all my named boxes and folders stacked on open shelves provide me with an index! Lest any reader ever visits me, I immediately confess that my study does not look like the inside of a filing cabinet, with everything straight and regimented! But everything does have its label, and everything does have its name in large letters that can be seen at a glance.

New file
'New file' is the first option when I scroll down on file, and so it should be. Creating a new file, of any sort, is to

be proactive. It's to make a decision to do something. Every new day is like a new file, yet sometimes we lose the benefit of its newness by seeing it merely as a continuation of what has gone before. God's Word says, 'This is the day the Lord has made; let us rejoice and be glad in it' (Ps. 118:24). The psalmist has made a decision; he has opened a file of rejoicing and gladness with which to celebrate the new day.

We have a handsome black Labrador called Sheba and she has three walks each day. Until recently my husband, Angus, took her out after breakfast and again at lunchtime. I took her a short walk late each afternoon, and I mean short as I walk with the aid of crutches or a walking frame. A few months ago Angus was unwell and I had to do all of Sheba's walks. When he recovered I persuaded him to change things round and leave me with the morning walk as I was enjoying it so much – and I'm not a morning person! This might not have been the case if our home was in a town or city. When we moved to Argyll on the west coast of Scotland, the verse, 'The boundary lines have fallen for me in pleasant places; surely I have a delightful inheritance' (Ps. 16:6) seemed to have been written especially for us.

Our home is just across the road from a sea loch, and the road along which Sheba and I wander weaves its way by the loch side. There's a wood on one side of the road and trees leading down to West Loch Tarbert on the other. The loch, which is just a few yards from the road, glints on sunny mornings and is splendidly exhilarating when the weather is rough. The wild flowers have to be seen to be believed. Primroses, buttoned into grass mats, bloom early and are followed by bluebells, wild garlic, cow parsley then red campion. And that's where we're at as I write this. The other day when Sheba and I were on our morning walk we found a bluebell (really a wild hyacinth) with thirty-three bells dangling from its stem. It was so heavily laden that its tip was nearly bent down to the ground. Overwhelmed by the beauty of it, I phoned a friend and asked her to come out from the village and enjoy it with me. Now, I still would have found it had I taken Sheba out later in the day. But the difference was this – that early morning encounter with such a delightful part of God's creation set the tone for my whole day. It was as though I was seeing things more clearly just because I looked at them with more appreciative eyes.

George Wade Robinson, the hymn-writer, expressed the thought beautifully.

> Heaven above is softer blue,
> Earth around is sweeter green;
> Something lives in every hue,
> Christless eyes have never seen:
> Birds with gladder songs o'erflow,
> Flowers with deeper beauties shine,
> Since I know, as now I know,
> I am his, and he is mine.

Being proactive in terms of personal organisation is, of course, not always easy. So many things gather around us that are just one-offs. And the thing with 'one-offs' is that they build up and clutter our lives. Some years ago I worked with London City Mission on two books, and for a week each month of the project I shared an office with Dr John Nicholls, now the L.C.M.'s Chief Executive. I learned many things from John, and one was that he cleared his in-tray nearly every day – even if he sometimes cleared it by recycling what was in it back to his secretary! He told me that when he did so not everything reappeared the following day. I don't have a secretary. Instead I have a box file labelled 'Bits & Bobs' and that's where things go until I decide whether or not they need a more permanent place in my life. It's just a regular box file, and I decide what needs to be kept and what needs to be discarded when the box will no longer close!

Close file
When my Bits & Bobs box file won't close (which happens every few months) I know that the time has come to make decisions. Does that newspaper clipping that seemed so interesting six weeks ago really need to be kept? Is the nice thank-you card I received now a part of me? Could I find five minutes to copy the recipe a friend gave me into my recipe book? And what about the diet tips I cut from a magazine? Have I applied them? Will I apply them? Then why are they taking up space in my life? The Bits & Bobs file is where I keep temporary things: the postal receipt until I know the package has arrived, the holiday booking information that will be discarded when we come home, the letters I just might decide to keep for sentimental reasons and 'funnies' that will make me smile over and over again. When decision time is over the Bits & Bobs file closes tight.

Closure is something we seek in life, and not just in terms of files and folders. It is so easy to keep life-files open long after they have passed their sell-by date. Are we still troubled by years-old criticisms? Does a long-ago argument still colour a relationship? Have we kept an unkind letter (just to remind us how unkind it was)? Are we cluttering our lives with life-files that should have been consigned to the dustbin long ago? Harbouring hurts and nurturing disagreements should not be among the hobbies of Christian men and women, yet when we honestly search our hearts we sometimes find them lurking there.

God's Word makes it clear that arguments should be settled on the day they are begun, not filed away for future use. 'You were taught, with regard to your former way of life, to put off your old self, which is being corrupted by its deceitful desires; to be made new in the attitude of your minds; and to put on the new self, created to be like God in true righteousness and holiness. Therefore each of you must put off falsehood and speak truthfully to his neighbour, for we are all members of one body. "In your anger do not sin." Do not let the sun go down while you are still angry, and do not give the devil a foothold. He who has been stealing must steal no longer ...' (Eph. 4:22-28). According to Scripture, keeping hurtful life-files open is right there among lying and stealing. Not only that, we are specifically told that it gives the devil a foothold in our lives!

Of course, we feel that if only others knew what we know, if only they'd heard what was said or read what was written they'd understand why things still trouble us. The problem is that the quote from Ephesians is straight from God's Word, and God *does* know. The Bible allows for no get-out clauses. Peter tried one. 'Then Peter came to Jesus and asked, "Lord, how many times shall I forgive my brother when he sins against me? Up to seven times?" Jesus answered, "I tell you, not seven times, but seventy-seven times. Therefore ..."' (Matt. 18:21-23). If we ignore Jesus' 'therefore', we miss out on the major part of the Lord's reply to Peter.

Jesus' 'therefore' was the beginning of the parable of the unmerciful servant. The kingdom of heaven, the Lord said, is like a king who wanted to settle his accounts with his servants. A servant who owed the king a substantial amount of money was unable to pay. He, along with his wife and children, was to be sent to prison and their possessions sold to repay the debt. When the servant begged for mercy, however, the king relented and cancelled the entire debt. Soon afterwards the forgiven servant came upon a man who owed him a small sum of money. He too was unable to pay. Notwithstanding what had happened to him, the servant had his debtor thrown into prison. When the king heard he was furious. "I cancelled all that debt of yours because you begged me to. Shouldn't you have had mercy on your fellow servant just as I had on you?" In anger his master turned him over to the jailors ... until he should pay back all he owned.' That's Jesus' parable; his application follows. 'This is how my heavenly Father will treat each of you unless you forgive your brother from your heart' (from Matt. 18:33-35). Jesus makes it quite clear that those who are forgiven must be forgiving. There is no place for keeping files open that should be closed. And one splendid thing about closing the files of hurt and anger is that our lives are less cluttered without them.

Delete file

After several years of using a word processor it became suddenly urgent that I learn to use a personal computer, scanner etc. Although that was ten years ago, I can still remember the feeling of panic. Much to my surprise, my denomination appointed me editor of *The Instructor*, its monthly magazine for four to twelve year-old children.

The appointment was made in May and the first issue for which I was responsible was due out that September – but had to be at the printer by the end of July. Panic! Fortunately our daughters were home for the summer and they supervised a crash course in computing. Like many adult learners I was scared in case I deleted something important that could not be retrieved. No matter how often the family assured me that wasn't possible, I treated the delete key as a total no-go area. I've since discovered that our daughters were perhaps more reassuring than totally honest! And my more up-to-date computer with its recycle bin, from which deleted documents can be retrieved, is reassuring.

How thankful I am that my heavenly Father does not have a recycle bin. 'Who is a God like you, who pardons sin and forgives the transgression of the remnant of his inheritance? You do not stay angry for ever but delight to show mercy. You will again have compassion on us; you will tread our sins underfoot and hurl all our iniquities into the depths of the sea' (Micah 7:18-19). A friend told me that she pictures her forgiven sins in the depths of the sea, and above them floats a marker buoy with the words 'No fishing!' painted on its side. Not only are our sins forgiven, they are deleted from the memory of the God against whom we have sinned. We have his word for that. '… I will forgive their wickedness and will remember their sins no more' (Jer. 31:34). Our forgiven sins have been deleted by our great and merciful God through the death of the Lord Jesus Christ on the cross. And when we wonder if perhaps he keeps them in a kind of celestial recycle bin to use in evidence against us at some future time, we need to remember that that is to doubt both the Word of God and the efficacy of the death of our Saviour.

Not only is Christ our Saviour, he is also our example and it should be the Christian's great desire and aim to imitate him. But when it comes to the deletion of other people's sins, how hard that is. Forgiveness is a difficult subject. Using God as our pattern, I conclude that true forgiveness is only possible when the person who has done wrong seeks forgiveness from the person wronged. Scripture nowhere teaches that God forgives everyone, quite the contrary. 'If we claim to be without sin, we deceive ourselves and the truth is not in us. *If we confess our sins*, he [God] is faithful and just and will forgive us our sins and purify us from all unrighteousness' (1 John 1:8-9, my emphasis).

Confession and forgiveness go hand in hand. Does that mean that when we are wronged we cannot forgive those who wrong us unless they confess and apologise? Yes, I think it does. Does it follow that we have to live with the burden – and it can indeed be a burden – of not having forgiven someone, perhaps for the rest of our lives. No, I don't think that follows. It seems to me, and I know that there are those whose opinion differs from mine on this matter, that we can have a spirit of forgiveness that is just waiting for the opportunity of expression. Even if that opportunity never presents itself, the fact of our willingness to forgive releases us from our burden. Perhaps this has something to say to those whose hurts were caused by people who are no longer alive.

Where do we put what hurts and upsets us? What do we do with those things that remind us of past wrongs done against us? If they are in the form of letters or e-mails there is no better place than the ultimate delete system – the shredder. Twenty years ago I suffered in an accident that resulted in continuing pain and my walking with the aid of crutches. I kept a diary over the most difficult years along with medical letters and the like. For a very long time these papers lay in the bottom drawer of my filing cabinet. I never looked at them, I wasn't tempted to do so, but they were there. In case of what? I really don't know. Two or three years ago, when I was doing some serious cleaning, I came across the familiar brown envelopes. And I can still remember the feeling of release – exhilaration, even – when I shredded them one by one without reading them first. The past was past, and it was best deleted from my life, even from the dark recesses of my filing cabinet.

3

SAVE = FOR POSTERITY

While some things are best deleted from our lives – and from our computer systems, cupboards and drawers – there are others that deserve to be kept. When our daughters were little my late mother spent a great deal of time with them. They did all kinds of things together, some that it was best I knew nothing about! On one occasion Mum and the girls wrote poems and drew pictures that were gathered up in an exercise book. Mum persuaded me to include one or two poems I'd written in the collection. I treasure that simple notebook and a companion volume of stories they made up together and Mum wrote down.

Another treasure reaches far back in time. When I was a child my mother showed me a worn cardboard box containing some old embroideries. It was only when I reached my teen years that I realised their significance. They were samplers worked by my grandmother, great-grandmother and great great-grandmother. In their day samplers were made by girls at school to demonstrate their proficiency in sewing, an important skill in those days of make do and mend. As my great great-grandmother was born in

1827, her sampler was probably stitched around 1840. I persuaded my mother to make one and my youngest daughter and I have also added to the set. All six have been framed and I hope they will be saved for future generations.

Other things deserve to be kept too, little bits and pieces that are part of us. Among my saved treasures (yes, they are in a labelled file!) can be found: children's drawings, family letters, special wedding invitations, an obituary of a dear friend that really caught his character, and a collection of 'funnies', copies of which I give to friends from time to time. These have no monetary value whatever, but they are of value to me. Which parent could possibly discard the letter from which the following is an extract? It was written by our middle daughter and sent to her older sister who had just gone away to university, for her to delete what was inapplicable and send back home.

I am fine / ill / dead / alive.
I am / am not settling at university.
I am enjoying / hating / loving being a student.
I have made one / none / many / few / hundreds of friend(s).
I am bored / excited / thrilled / frightened by my lecturers.
They are nice / nasty / exciting / boring. I am loved by nobody / everybody in Dundee.
On Sunday I went to the Free Church / Church of Scotland / APC / Brethren / Baptist Church / Episcopal Church / Catholic Church / Synagogue / Mosque / all of these / none of these.

Some little things are of such significance to me that they are kept in a special place; they are stuck into a book labelled 'Counting my Blessings.' My grandmother taught me the old song, 'Count your blessings, name them one by one. Count your blessings, see what God has done. Count your blessings, name them one by one, and it will surprise you what the Lord has done.' What simple words, but what a profound sentiment. How often we accept God's blessings yet hardly allow them to impinge on our consciousness. A new day, birdsong, a child's smile, health and strength, the meeting of our daily needs, the last breath we took as we read this. But there are some special blessings, and it is these I keep in 'Counting my Blessings.' Let me tell you about some of them.

'Counting my Blessings' contains an e-mail from Christian Focus telling me that two of my children's books were to be translated into Russian, and one letting me know that another book was to be made into an audio cassette for Torch Trust for the Blind. There is also a page that records my gratitude to the Lord for preserving my oldest friend. Helen and I were at school together and we have been close ever since. Our lives have been very different. While I married and had three children at home here in Scotland, Helen became a missionary in Pakistan where she served the Lord in Sialkot then Gujranwala. On 5th August 2002, Angus and I were heading out for a meal to celebrate his birthday. As we drove, we listened to the news on the car radio. To our horror we heard that Murree Christian School in Pakistan – where we knew Helen was spending the summer – had been attacked by gunmen and that there were fatalities. It was several days before we knew our friend was safe. The few words that record the event in 'Counting my Blessings' don't even begin to express my gratitude for God's preservation of her precious life. But in years to come, when I read through the book, what's there will remind me of God's blessing that day.

In Victorian times many British women kept common-place books. They were usually notebooks in which the common-place things of life were recorded. Glancing through a common-place book (and some are to be found in libraries) gives a lovely insight into a woman's life. Some things commonly included were drawings done by children, funeral notice cards, Scripture verses that had meant something special, the points of a sermon that spoke to the heart, family births, weddings and deaths, the first words spoken by children, the last words spoken on a death-bed, letters, the favourite recipe of each member of a family, pressed flowers and little bits of fabric from home-made clothes, especially those worn on significant occasions. Christian women who kept common-place books generally wrote a short account of their testimony for posterity.

Imagine that you've come home from a hard day's work. You're tired and you have a full evening ahead. The garden's waiting to be done and some letters need writing. There are calls to be made, homework to be supervised and much else beside. The telephone rings. When you answer it, you hear an excited voice at the other end. It's your cousin, and unaware of your tiredness and how much you have to do, she launches off in her excitement. 'I was spring-cleaning in the attic today, and you'll never guess what I found! It's a sort of scrapbook our great-grandmother kept. It's full of all kinds of interesting things! There's a lock of our grandmother's baby hair and your mother's favourite pudding recipe when she was a little girl! And guess what, she drew out the design for the embroidery on the family christening gown in the book, the one your children wore when they were baptised! I'd always wondered who made it.'

How would you react to a call like that? Would you excuse yourself on account of the gardening? Would you explain that there were letters waiting to be written and you'd hear about the dusty old book another day? I think not! I think you'd make an arrangement to see your cousin as soon as possible and you'd pore over the common-place book together with growing fascination. Now, imagine that you were brought up going to church but lost interest in your teen years and have only been back for weddings and baptisms since then. Think of the impact that reading your great-grandmother's Christian testimony might have upon you. That really would be a case of speaking from beyond the grave. We have scriptural precedent for that. 'Now faith is being sure of what we hope for and certain of what we do not see. This is what the ancients were commended for. By faith we understand that the universe was formed at God's command, so that what is seen was not made out of what was visible. By faith Abel offered God a better sacrifice than Cain did. By faith he was commended as a righteous man, when God spoke well of his offerings. And by faith *he still speaks, even though he is dead'* (Heb. 11:1-4, emphasis mine). We pray for our children and our grandchildren. The effort of making a common-place book might be richly rewarded. It could speak to our children, our grandchildren, and future generations that we can't imagine, in ways that might do their souls eternal good. Our great God is able to do that. I confess that I have not yet begun to make a common-place book but I think I have now been challenged into doing so.

4

SAVE = FOR ETERNITY

However dear *things* are to us, however much we want them saved for posterity, there is nothing more precious than the souls of those we love. There is nothing we long for with greater yearning than that their souls will be saved. Most Christian parents pray for their children from before they are born, and their prayers are their daily joy and their daily burden till the end of their lives. They know the Lord Jesus cares for their children, however young they are. 'People were bringing little children to Jesus to have him touch them, but the disciples rebuked them. When Jesus saw this, he was indignant. He said to them, "Let the little children come to me, and do not hinder them, for the kingdom of God belongs to such as these"' (Mark 10:13-14).

Using scripture as their guide, believing parents try to bring up their sons and daughters in the knowledge and awe of the Lord. 'Hear, O Israel: The LORD our God, the LORD is one. Love the LORD your God with all your heart and with all your soul and with all your strength. These commandments that I give you today are to be upon your hearts. Impress them on your children. Talk about them when you sit at home and when you walk along the road, when you lie down and when you get up' (Deut. 6:4-7). 'Great is the Lord and most worthy of praise; his greatness no-one can fathom. One generation will commend your works to another; they will tell of your mighty acts. They will speak of the glorious splendour of your majesty, and I will meditate on your wonderful works' (Ps. 145:3-5).

Conscious of our ignorance, we take parenting lessons from the Word of our own Father in heaven. 'Trust in the Lord with all your heart and lean not on your own understanding; in all your ways acknowledge him, and he will make your paths straight' (Prov. 3:5-6). 'Discipline your son, and he will give you peace; he will bring delight to your soul' (Prov. 29:17). 'Fathers, do not exasperate your children; instead, bring them up in the training and instruction of the Lord' (Eph. 6:4). 'Fathers, do not embitter your children, or they will become discouraged' (Col. 3:21).

Parents answer the questions posed to them in a way that shows God's purposes. 'He [Joshua] said to the Israelites, "In the future, when your descendants ask their fathers, 'What do these stones mean?' tell them, 'Israel crossed the Jordan on dry ground.' For the Lord your God dried up the Jordan before you until you had crossed over. The Lord your God did to the Jordan just what he had done to the Red Sea when he dried it up before us until we had crossed over. He did this so that all the peoples of the earth might know that the hand of the Lord is powerful and so that you might always fear the Lord your God"' (Josh. 4:21-24).

As our young people grow up we try to base our advice to them on biblical teaching and standards. 'My son, pay attention to what I say: listen closely to my words. Do not let them out of your sight, keep them within your heart; for they are life to those who find them and health to a man's whole body. Above all else, guard your heart, for it is the wellspring of life. Put away perversity from your mouth; keep corrupt talk far from your lips' (Prov. 4:20-24). And Scripture is nothing if not practical in the advice it gives to parents to pass on to their children. 'Listen, my son, and be wise; and keep your heart on the right path. Do not join those who drink too much wine or gorge themselves on meat, for drunkards and gluttons become poor, and drowsiness clothes them in rags' (Prov. 23:19-21). In our day of 'how to' books, the Book of Proverbs could be promoted as the Bible's 'How to be a parent' textbook!

Believing parents cling to God's promises, often marking them in their Bibles in order to find them quickly. '...From everlasting to everlasting the Lord's love is with those who fear him, and his righteousness with their children's children – with those who keep his covenant and remember to obey his precepts' (Ps. 103:17-18). 'Repent and be baptised, every one of you, in the name of Jesus Christ for the forgiveness of your sins. And you will receive the gift of the Holy Spirit. The promise is for you and your children and for all who are far off – for all whom the Lord our God will call' (Acts 2:38-39). 'Train a child in the way he should go, and when he is old he will not turn from it' (Prov. 22:6).

Our children are at home with us for what feels like a few short years (looking back!) before making their own way in the world. Parents who have the inestimable privilege of seeing their young people going on in the faith are truly blessed. Others wait and pray, still holding on to God's promises. 'Those who sow in tears will reap with songs of joy. He who goes out weeping, carrying seed to sow, will return with songs of joy, carrying sheaves with him' (Ps. 126:5-6). The godly Job is the Bible's example of a man whose adult children were still upheld by his prayers. 'His sons used to take turns holding feasts in their homes, and they would invite their three sisters to eat and drink with them. When a period of feasting had run its course, Job would send and have them purified. Early in the morning he would sacrifice a burnt offering for each of them, thinking, "Perhaps my children have sinned and cursed God in their hearts." This was Job's regular custom' (Job 1:4-5).

Many Christian parents, who see their adult children turn their backs on the faith, are left in a state of confusion. Although they are very conscious of all their failings, they've done their best. They love their children and their deepest desire for them is that they should be saved. But they cannot save them. Our adult children are responsible to God, are answerable to God. King David ensured that his son, the wise Solomon, understood this to be true. 'And you, my son Solomon, acknowledge the God of your father, and serve him with wholehearted devotion and with a willing mind, for the Lord searches every heart and understands every motive behind the thoughts. If you seek him, he will be found by you; but if you forsake him, he will reject you forever' (1 Chron. 28:9). Surely the Christian parent's prayer is that their children seek the Lord and are found by him, that they do not forsake him and be rejected.

Several years ago I heard a sermon that I know deeply affected many who heard it, for there were those in the congregation whose children had not darkened the door of a church for many years. The preacher spoke from John 20:19-20. 'On the evening of that first day of the week, when the disciples were together, with the doors locked for fear of the Jews, Jesus came and stood among them and said, "Peace be with you!" After he said this, he showed them his hands and side. The disciples were overjoyed when they saw the Lord.' By way of encouragement, the preacher reminded his hearers that God is sovereign. Closed hearts are no more of a barrier to Jesus than are closed doors. Although Christian parents may think their adult children's hearts are closed hard against the Lord, he is able to penetrate the hardness, to proclaim peace to them, to show them what he did for them on the cross and to fill them with the joy of salvation. God is sovereign. God is able!

We have all known dear Christian parents who have gone to their graves knowing that their children are unsaved, parents who have wondered for many years what they did wrong. Where did they fail? What could they have done better? Satan, always the opportunist, then insinuates the obvious conclusion – it's all your fault. It might shed just a little light into that darkness to realise the implication of the devil's insinuation. If our adult children's rejection of the faith is because of mistakes we have made in their upbringing, it follows that if we had made fewer mistakes they would now be believers. But that is to say that *we* are responsible for our children's salvation, that our parenting skill is what makes our children trust in the Lord! Put like that, it is clearly absurd. Salvation is all of Jesus, and that truth sheds a comforting glow in the darkness. If the Lord waited until hearts were open before moving in people's lives, there would not be a single believer on the face of the earth.

Jonathan and Sarah Edwards, both most godly and most influential Christians, had a large family. Their children were brought up right in the middle of the Great Awakening in eighteenth-century New England. The Holy Spirit worked in a wonderful way at that time and their children saw hundreds of those they knew being converted or revived. Both Jonathan and Sarah died relatively young, but they must have been overjoyed to see their children come, one after the other, to saving faith. And from that couple alone has come a veritable dynasty of Christians. By 1900 they had an astounding 1,400 descendants! Among them were over a hundred missionaries along with ministers, professors, lawyers, doctors, politicians and businessmen. But their very own grandson, both of whose parents were devoted to the Lord, was 'a disaster in emotional and moral terms' despite rising to the very highest echelons of United States politics.

Recently I edited a manuscript which told a very different story. A young man's parents separated before he could remember and he was brought up by a father who came and went and his partner who abused him terribly. There was nothing of the love of the Lord in that boy's upbringing. He wasn't put to bed at night with a Bible story and prayer. He didn't see conversions happening all around him. There was no queue of people at his door wanting to speak to his father in order to know how to be saved. He was a no-hoper when he met a group of young Christians, and he told them very firmly that he wasn't interested in the faith they were peddling. But the young Christians persisted, even travelling a long way to visit him in prison. They were there for him on his release, providing a home and praying for him and with him. That young man did become a Christian and he's now a missionary working with street children in South America. God is sovereign.

Save as

One temptation open to Christian parents is to try to push their children into full-time Christian service in the mistaken belief that that's how they should serve the Lord. Their prayer is sometimes a 'save as' prayer. 'Please save my son as a preacher, my daughter as a missionary.' But to do that is to demean any other kind of work. It does us good to remember that the Lord Jesus himself was a carpenter, that his hands were roughened by hard work. Neither did Paul have the hands of an aesthete. '... Paul ... went to Corinth. There he met a Jew named Aquila, a native of Pontus, who had recently come from Italy with his wife Priscilla. ...Paul went to see them, and because *he was a tentmaker as they were, he stayed and worked with them*' (Acts 18:1-3, emphasis mine). And he did not give up his trade to become a paid preacher. Even though he teaches that '... the Lord has commanded that those who preach the gospel should receive their living from the gospel' (1 Cor. 9:14), it is clear that Paul also had a secular job. Of course Christians are in the Lord's service full-time whatever their job. The teacher, mother, fisherman, secretary, lawyer, street sweeper and hairdresser are all in full-time Christian jobs if a Christian is doing them. Our prayers for our children should be for their salvation rather than being 'save as' prayers. God will lead them in the way he wants them to go.

Save a copy

There are three options regarding saving on my computer: save, save as, and save a copy. Sadly some of us try to save ourselves as a copy of someone we know and admire. Perhaps this is especially true of inexperienced preachers. Every preacher has his own little idiosyncrasies: a certain way of holding his head, his own way of pronouncing particular words, a style of dress, the rise and fall of his voice as he preaches. When I was a young teenager my minister, who meant a great deal to me, clasped his hands with his left thumb on top. Try it; it doesn't come naturally to most people. In my childishness, clasping my hands as he did made me feel very pious! It's in the catching of these little things that mimics make their subjects instantly recognisable.

Preachers have to find their own style. A young man cloning himself on a well-known preacher is rather a sad sight. Everyone knows – apart from the young man – that he should be himself; he should be as God made him. But what we sometimes forget is that our children should be themselves; they should be as God made them. It is not for us to try to mould them into someone we admire and respect, even a famous Christian. God's Word says, 'Be imitators of God, therefore, as dearly loved children and live a life of love, just as Christ loved us and gave himself up for us as a fragrant offering and sacrifice to God' (Eph. 5:1). And when Paul said, 'I urge you to imitate me,' it was with respect to 'my way of life in Christ Jesus, which agrees with what I teach everywhere in every church' (1 Cor. 4:16-17), not in his God-given individuality. Our job as parents is not to try to produce clones of ourselves (horror of horrors!), nor to nurture our children as clones of any other human being, however admirable, but to encourage them from their tenderest years to imitate God as seen in the Lord Jesus Christ.

5

PRINT

When I was about four years old my uncle and aunt left Scotland to start a new life in Canada. I remember my distress at saying goodbye to him because Uncle Jim was a kind and gentle man and I loved him very much. He and Aunt Susie went by boat and had several days at sea. One morning, while en route, Uncle Jim lit a cigarette and had a sudden urge to give up smoking. 'I'm going to give this up, God help me,' he said to his wife. But there was no thought of God helping or otherwise. Uncle Jim wasn't a Christian, and that was just an expression plucked out of the air. That night, when he was emptying his trouser pockets, he discovered he'd not smoked a single cigarette since morning. Remembering the words he had spoken, he knew that God had indeed helped him. Within days Uncle Jim and Aunt Susie began a new life twice over – they found new life in Jesus Christ as they began their new life in Canada as Christians.

Although I had not started school I was able to read and write, thanks to a brother seven years my senior. Uncle Jim knew that, and he decided to write to this little girl left at home and tell her about the Lord Jesus. All through my childhood and teens Uncle Jim wrote; he also sent tracts and daily Bible reading notes. And I know he prayed for me. Each time they came home on a visit Uncle Jim and Aunt Susie talked to me about the Lord. How I looked forward to their first visit back after my conversion when I was sixteen years old!

When I became editor of *The Instructor*, I encouraged the children who read it to write to me, and they do ... by the hundred! A few write almost every month, and most of their letters are just what you would expect from small children. But over the years I've developed relationships with many of them, and some who are now student age still write to me. In every reply I say a little about the Lord, and I don't mean a sermon. For example, I might tell them that if they learn something new and wonderful about Jesus every day of their life and live to be a hundred, they will still have amazing new things to learn about him in heaven. It takes minutes to write such a letter, but I know from my Uncle Jim that those minutes are invested in eternity.

Is letter-writing a dying art? I do hope not. A letter can reach where a phone call or e-mail cannot. However heart-warming a phone call is, it can only be heard once. A letter can be picked up over and over again and warm the recipient's heart each time. There's many a parent who still has all the letters their children have written to them. I wonder if many keep their e-mails. I once heard how even empty envelopes had a heart-warming effect on the woman to whom they were sent. In the mid nineteenth century a young man left the Western Isles of Scotland for America. He could neither read nor write, and certainly not in English. When he arrived in the New World and found a job he asked his employer to write his widowed mother's name and address on an envelope which he then posted to her. That empty envelope was treasured by his mother because she knew her son was alive and well. About once a year thereafter he sent an empty envelope home. Then, when he was in middle age, he made the effort to learn to read and write. From then on he laboriously wrote a short letter to put in the annual envelope. When his mother died all that he had ever sent her was found tied together and kept beside her Bible. And the letters he had written over the last years of her life had gone unread. The envelopes were still sealed; it had never occurred to her to open them.

A letter is a gift. Think how you feel when you find a personal letter among your clutter of mail. Doesn't it feel good? And when you recognise that the handwriting belongs to someone you love, you even savour opening it. When I'm hurtling towards a deadline I sometimes leave mail unopened for a week or more – but not personal letters. No more would I leave a gift lying unwrapped! And letters are gifts *we* can give. They don't need to be long; they just need to be. One of my elderly friends is housebound and she has a real ministry in terms of letter writing. She writes when she knows we're under pressure, to welcome us back from holidays, to assure us of her prayers and just to tell us she loves us. She has a beautiful ministry.

Women sometimes complain of being undervalued in the church. They can feel that men do all the ministry things and they are relegated to the kitchen, the crèche, and the primary Sunday school. Yet there is a ministry of letter-writing just waiting for them to buy notelets and postage stamps. Looking back over the years I can identify times when letters were especially precious to me.

- When I was a young Christian taking the first steps in the faith.
- When I left home for the first time.
- When I started teaching, and what a scary experience that was!
- When I was a stay-at-home mum.
- When the children started school.
- When they left for university.
- When we moved into a new area of ministry.
- When I became unable to walk.
- More recently, when my husband was ill for some time.
- When I'm reaching a deadline on a book.

And as I wrote that list I realised how many people I know who might be blessed if I were to take time right now and write some letters.

Clipboard

What could be more different from writing personal letters than a clipboard! The first is warm and caring while the second is official and sometimes officious. Some years ago, when I was in hospital, I heard myself being referred to as 'the ankle in bed 8'. I wrote a poem about that and, not surprisingly called it 'The Clipboard.' Whipthorpe felt like a good name to call the doctor concerned, though his was something quite different.

You bore down on me
Dr Whipthorpe
ready for battle
armour – white coat
I D – stethoscope
Weapon – clipboard.
I fought
to prise personality
from starched cotton,
struggled to show
the machine tested
was me.

But you won,
I'd no chance;
the clipboard did it.

Wounded,
I watched you throw it down,
heard the thud,
the ricochet.

Your parting shot
aimed at the nurse
hit me
'That's the ankle,'
it rang out,
'in bed 8.'

What is it that makes us change from a person into
a position? Perhaps it has sometimes to do with insecurity,
or a need to be recognised for what we are rather than who
we are. Sometimes that's no bad thing. When Paul's God-
given authority as an apostle was challenged in Corinth,
he listed his credentials for all to read. 'Are they Hebrews?

So am I. Are they Israelites? So am I. Are they Abraham's descendants? So am I. Are they servants of Christ? (I am out of my mind to talk like this.) I am more. I have worked much harder, been in prison more frequently, been flogged more severely, and been exposed to death again and again. ...' (2 Cor. 11:22-23).

Paul lists the dangers through which he has gone for the Lord before going on to outline his spiritual credentials. Then, lest they think him proud, Paul tells the Corinthians just how human and frail he is. 'To keep me from becoming conceited because of these surpassingly great revelations, there was given me a thorn in my flesh, a messenger of Satan, to torment me. Three times I pleaded with the Lord to take it away from me. But he said to me, "My grace is sufficient for you, for my power is made perfect in weakness." Therefore I will boast all the more gladly about my weaknesses, so that Christ's power may rest on me. That is why, for Christ's sake, I delight in weaknesses, in insults, in hardships, in persecutions, in difficulties. For when I am weak, then I am strong' (2 Cor. 12:7-10). Paul's conclusion is revealing. 'I have made a fool of myself, *but you drove me to it*. I ought to have been commended by you, for I am not in the least inferior to the "super-apostles", even though I am nothing' (v. 11, emphasis mine).

The apostle was *driven* to having to establish his authority. Far from seeking power for the sake of power, he was seeking authority for the sake of the gospel. And that should not have been necessary because he displayed the 'signs, wonders and miracles' that were the mark of an apostle (v. 12). Clipboard-style officiousness was not one of the marks of apostleship! And neither is it a mark of a Christian. As Paul's life was testimony to what he was, so our lives should be testimony to what we are – without us boasting about our credentials and demanding respect. If we are Christians, do we live Christianly? If we are parents, do we exert loving authority? If we are in the ministry, do we remember we are called there by Christ and that in and of ourselves we, like Paul, are nothing? If we are in secular employment, do we remember that we are Christ's representatives there? If we are in positions of authority, do we respect those under us, remembering that they too are made in the image of Almighty God, no matter how menial the job they are paid to do?

I do have a clipboard. It sits beside my computer and I keep my monthly working time-sheet on it. From time to time when I look at it I think of Dr Whipthorpe. Without his white coat, stethoscope and clipboard he was just an ordinary man. I may have written a number of books, but without Christ I am nothing, absolutely nothing.

6

COPY

When I was in my early twenties a friend gave me a rather unusual birthday present, an ancient Gestetner duplicator. Using it was an enormously messy procedure. First the document had to be typed out on to a paper-backed 'skin'. The keys of the typewriter cut through the skin so making a stencil through which ink would flow. Then thick ink pressed from a metal tube was spread on to the Gestetner's rollers and the stencil put in position – an operation no less intricate than applying very fine wallpaper! Tearing the stencil or creasing it was all too easy. That completed, the paper was put in and the amazing machine rattled and cranked through the production of as many copies as I wanted. Those brought up with modern high-tech photocopiers don't know the half of it! Now multiple copies are churned out over a cup of coffee.

The copying that concerns Christians is their desire to copy Jesus, to be more like their Saviour day by day. It is awesome to know that in heaven we will be like the Lord, yet we know that to be true. 'Dear friends, now we are children of God, and what we will be has not yet been made known.

But we know that when he appears, we shall be like him, for we shall see him as he is' (1 John 3:2). But we cannot leave it until eternity to begin to be like Jesus. As John goes on to say, 'Everyone who has this hope in him purifies himself, just as he [Jesus] is pure' (v. 3). How wonderful it would be if we were made like Christ at the moment of our conversion, but how soon we know we are not. Satan lurks beside believers, delighting in each successful temptation, each victory won. What a comfort it is to know that the eternal victory has been won on the cross at Calvary, and that we live in the age of the death throes of Satan. Yes, he can tempt us. Yes, we will at times fall and fail. But no, he cannot rob us of our salvation. He may lurk at our side but we are utterly safe. Jesus said, 'I give them eternal life, and they shall never perish; no-one can snatch them out of my hand' (John 10:28).

Copy – Jesus in prayer
With our destiny secure, we set out each new day to copy Jesus. He is our example of Christian living, our pattern. Christ's prayer life is given that we might copy it. Jesus prayed at the beginning of the day. 'Very early in the morning, while it was still dark, Jesus got up, left the house and went off to a solitary place, where he prayed' (Mark 1:35). For many of us the beginning of the day is frenetic. 'Time to get up!' 'We're running late!' 'Someone fill the kettle while I put out the cereal.' 'Are the packed lunches made?' 'Have the children taken their gym kit … dinner money … bus fares?' And all of this with the radio blasting out news in the background, or the television beaming it from the corner of the room. Quiet time? The very idea of spending time with the Lord at the beginning of the day is enough to send most parents on a guilt trip!

It was after our children had grown up and left home that I learned a morning lesson that has helped me. Previously my first action on going into the kitchen was to switch on the radio to catch up with what was happening in the world. But one day something my husband said in a sermon really hit home. 'Why is it,' Angus asked, 'that so many of us want to hear the voice of man each morning before we listen to the voice of God?' All of our married life it has been our practice to read a passage from the Bible and pray after breakfast. As we read, we look in God's Word for what HE has to say for the day. Angus's question made me realise that I was plugging myself into what the world had to say before considering what God was saying. The radio is now silent until after we've worshipped the One who gives each new morning.

My special time of quietness and prayer in the morning is after we've had worship together when I set out for a walk with the dog. Each day I ask God to show me something special as I walk along the loch side. The other day he showed me a foxglove growing behind a bush on the roadside. Just a tiny patch of purple showing through the bush pointed me to the beautiful flower. But I was able to get near it and look at its perfection. And as I held one of its 'gloves' and looked inside it my heart filled with worship. In any day perhaps only six people walk along our single-track road, and it may be that none of them even noticed the hidden foxglove. I felt as though God had taken me aside to show me something that he had made for my own personal enjoyment.

The following morning the wind rose as I walked. I was just enjoying the feel of it on my face when God showed me some long grass in seed swaying in the wind. It was exquisite! Even Fabergé could not have equalled its delicacy!

There was still a suggestion of dew on the seed-heads and the morning sun made them glisten as they swayed. I took one stalk and ran it through my fingers for the sheer pleasure of touching such beauty. And I worshipped the One who placed it there and who pointed it out to me in order that I, like him, could look at what he had made and know that it is very good.

Yesterday as Sheba and I walked along the side of the loch, God pointed me to the lowest branch of a beech tree. I stopped and held the end of the branch the better to look at the leaves. The smallest one had the softness of baby skin. It almost made me tingle to touch it. Just behind it was a slightly bigger leaf, a little deeper in colour and more substantial to touch. Turning it over, I marvelled at the intricacy of its structure. Behind it was a third leaf almost full-grown. It felt hardy and business-like, ready to withstand whatever weather came upon it, and quite prepared to hang on in there until autumn. Worship is different when you hold in your hand something beautiful God made, something he pointed out to you, something in which you and he share delight.

Now, I know that I am richly blessed in living in this beautiful part of southwest Scotland and that most people wake up to life in an urban environment with all the distractions that brings. Yet the sun still shines there, lighting up the dew-covered spider's web to make it more delicately beautiful than any diamond tiara. The rain still falls there, watering whatever growing things drink it up. Window boxes, gardens and parks are full of God's handiwork. If you ask our Creator God to show you something new every morning, you may find yourself led into worship by what he reveals.

Decision times

Scripture records that Jesus also prayed before making important decisions. 'One of those days Jesus went out into the hills to pray, and spent the night praying to God. When morning came, he called his disciples to him and chose twelve of them, whom he also designated apostles: Simon (whom he named Peter), his brother Andrew, James, John, Philip, Bartholomew, Matthew, Thomas, James son of Alphaeus, Simon who was called the Zealot, Judas son of James, and Judas Iscariot, who became a traitor' (Luke 6:12-16). It was important that Jesus got it right, that he chose those who had already been chosen from all eternity. Even the betrayer had to be chosen that day in order that God's great plan of salvation could be worked out in the life and death of Jesus. No wonder the Saviour spent the night in prayer.

Do decisions send us to prayer or drive us to distraction? Is worry our first response to having to make an important choice, or do we really cast our cares on the Lord and wait patiently for him? Perhaps Jesus' secret was his deep understanding of the fact that he was involved in the outworking of God's plan. When I was a young Christian one of my favourite choruses said:

> Oh the love that drew salvation's plan,
> Oh the grace that brought it down to man,
> Oh the mighty gulf that God did span at Calvary.
> Mercy there was great and grace was free,
> Pardon there was multiplied to me,
> There my burdened soul found liberty, at Calvary.

Jesus was involved in planning the salvation of his people. And at every step along the way – even when it involved appointing the one who was to betray him – he knew that he was doing his Father's will. His times of communion with his Father in prayer must have reassured him.

"'I know the plans I have for you," declares the Lord, "plans to prosper you and not to harm you, plans to give you hope and a future. Then you will call upon me and come and pray to me, and I will listen to you. You will seek me and find me when you seek me with all your heart. I will be found by you," declares the Lord, "and will bring you back from captivity. I will gather you from all the nations and places where I have banished you," declares the Lord, "and will bring you back to the place from which I carried you into exile"' (Jer. 29:11-14).

The truth is that God has plans for all his people, just as he had a plan for his Son. Our decisions are taken, as Jesus' decisions were taken, against the backdrop of God's perfect plan. We are not cast adrift to fend for ourselves, nor are we in uncharted territory. God already knows the whens, wheres and hows of our lives because he planned them. Should we not, therefore, seek his leading when decisions have to be taken rather than worrying ourselves into nervous exhaustion? If our lives are planned, then going to the One who made the plan seems much the most sensible thing to do.

I don't know if God told his Son the names of those who were to be apostles or whether, after spending time in communion with his Father, Jesus was left to use his own knowledge and discernment. Whichever it was, his time of prayer must have reassured him. And so it is with us. God has gifted us with common sense and the ability to reason and think things through. When we spend time in prayer prior to making decisions we are reassured.

7

Copy = Jesus' devotion

The Lord Jesus also sought God in prayer at times of distress. 'When Jesus heard what had happened [John the Baptist's murder], he withdrew by boat privately to a solitary place' (Matt. 14:13). How often we hear people cry out to God when tragedy strikes, even when they only normally use his name as a swear word. Believers also cry out in their distress, and they have biblical warrant to do so. David was in serious danger when he called on the Lord. 'Be merciful to me, O God, for men hotly pursue me; all day long they press their attack. My slanderers pursue me all day long; many are attacking me in their pride' (Ps. 56:1-2). But David cried out in assurance as well as distress. He went on to say, 'When I am afraid, I will trust in you. In God, whose word I praise, in God I trust; I will not be afraid. What can mortal man do to me?' (v. 3-4). That is the difference. When those who are strangers to God and to grace cry out in time of tragedy or danger, they do not cry to someone they know, someone in whom they trust, someone on whose word they rely, someone whose company takes away their fears. David hit the nail right on the head when he asked, 'What can mortal man do to me?' In the light of God's sovereign plan for our lives, mortal man can do nothing to us that God does not allow, nor can Satan. The first two chapters of the book of Job render that irrefutable.

Gethsemane

A day came in the life of Jesus when he was fearfully oppressed. He knew what was about to happen, that in just a few hours he would dredge the depths of what mortal man could do. And everything in him recoiled at the prospect of the cross, everything apart from his commitment to do his Father's will. Taking three friends for support, he went to the Garden of Gethsemane. Jesus 'withdrew about a stone's throw beyond them, knelt down and prayed, "Father, if you are willing, take this cup from me; yet not my will, but yours be done"' (Luke 22:41-42). And his friends slept just a few feet away. Thankfully we will never be called upon to go through Jesus' appalling experience that night. But there are times when such awful things happen that we truly struggle to see God's hand in then. Sadly sometimes our Christian friends are also at a loss and don't provide the support we need because they don't understand what's happening either. Jesus' prayer is then wrung from the believer's heart, 'Yet not my will, but yours be done.'

Over the years I've compiled several books of testimonies. A number of them contain accounts of Christian people who have been taken along very dark roads. One contributor shared the story of the murder of a cherished daughter, another told of living with severe psychiatric illness, yet another gave an account of being stuck in one physical position from the age of fourteen through Still's

Disease and therefore totally dependent on others to meet every single need on every single day of her life. Over the years of my life as a Christian writer I have sat for many, many hours listening to God's people talking about the most terrible experiences. Yet, in them all and through them all, they have said with the psalmist, '... I will yet praise him, my Saviour and my God' (Ps. 42:11).

In the course of writing one chapter I spent some hours with a friend talking about her life. Margaret's husband was in prison for a very serious offence and her mother's health was causing her concern. She herself was anticipating cardiac surgery to correct a long-term heart defect. Although that was some years ago, I can almost hear Margaret speaking. 'I still struggle at times with depression and loneliness – sometimes to the point when death seems a means of escape – but my times are in my Father's hands. I do not know the future regarding my marriage. ... Sometimes I feel overwhelmed by the pain of it all. ... Soon I will have further heart surgery, without which my quality of life would decrease quite markedly. I will commit myself into the skilful hands of an anaesthetist and a surgeon. I can do that with assurance, because I have already committed myself to the One who is able to do more than we ask or think, who will keep me to all eternity, and who has promised never to leave me nor forsake me, and to guide me safely to my eternal home. In Isaiah 43:1 (NIV) the Lord says. "Fear not, for I have redeemed you, I have called you by name; you are mine." And I believe him.'

Long before the book went to print my friend was safe in the nearer presence of Jesus in her eternal home. Margaret did not regain consciousness after her surgery and died a few days later. For her 'there will be no more death or mourning or crying or pain, for the old order of things has passed away' (Rev. 21:4). I learned several things from my friend, not least that, in times of real need and oppression, God was at her side, hearing and answering her prayers. And when the time came for Margaret's surgery, when her prayer was that God's will rather than hers be done, she went to sleep quietly and woke up in heaven.

Our example

In the Bible we find another aspect of Jesus' prayer life that stands as an example for us to copy, the fact that even in times of deep desire to be alone with his Father his compassion was such that he stepped aside to help those who were in need. 'When Jesus heard what had happened [John the Baptist's murder], he withdrew by boat privately to a solitary place. Hearing of this, the crowds followed him on foot from the towns. When Jesus landed and saw a large crowd, he had compassion on them and healed their sick' (Matt. 14:13-14). Then Jesus fed the crowd, all five thousand plus of them. Only then, 'Jesus made the disciples get into the boat and go on ahead of him to the other side, while he dismissed the crowd. After he had dismissed them, he went up on a mountainside by himself to pray' (Matt. 14:22-23).

Imagine what that must have been like. Jesus had just heard of the execution of John the Baptist, his forerunner, his cousin, the only one who understood him. The Lord, needing time with his Father, set out by boat to find somewhere lonely and quiet – and found a huge crowd desperate for his attention. Despite his grief, despite his yearning for solitude, Jesus turned aside for a considerable space of time in order to heal their sick and feed them all.

But the tidying up was no sooner completed than Jesus dismissed the crowd, sent his disciples off to their next port of call, and headed for the hills and a time with his heavenly Father. And this was no five minutes before lying down for a well-earned rest; Jesus was still praying some hours later (v. 25).

While it is, of course, good to follow a regular pattern in our devotional lives, are we sometimes less flexible than the One whose example we copy? Do we even on occasions use prayer as a way of 'doing our duty by someone' rather than being more practical in our Christian concern? I have to admit that it is considerably easier to ask God's blessings on some of those I love, especially those to whom I'm closest, than it is to actually speak to them about the Lord, just as it's easier to send them one of my books than it is to write a letter sharing something of my experience of God's grace. Jesus balanced his devotional life and his practical compassion in ways from which we have much to learn.

Committed

When Jesus prayed in Gethsemane he knew what was before him. The cross did not come as a fearful surprise to the author of the plan of salvation. The cross was why he came. But having done what he had to do there for the salvation of his people, the Redeemer prayed one more time. 'Jesus called out with a loud voice, "Father, into your hands I commit my spirit"' (Luke 23:46). The Jewish rulers and their Roman overlords did not snatch his life from him. When his work was fully completed, he committed his spirit to his Father in heaven then died.

It is not always given to us to know the time of our death. For some it comes suddenly and quite unexpectedly, with no time for the spirit to be committed to God. It is well for those whose every day is committed to the Lord, for they are always ready to die. I had the inestimable privilege of spending the last week of an elderly aunt's life with her. She was ninety-three years old and she knew she was dying. In fact, after I had sat with her for three or four days and nights she told me that she hadn't realised it would take so long to die. The waiting was hard. I read to her, prayed with her, and sang some of her favourite hymns as we waited. The hymn that seemed to speak most deeply to her was a paraphrase of 1 Peter 1:3-5.

> Bless'd be the everlasting God,
> the Father of our Lord;
> Be his abounding mercy prais'd,
> his majesty ador'd.
>
> When from the dead he rais'd his Son,
> and call'd him to the sky,
> He gave our souls a lively hope
> that they should never die.
>
> To an inheritance divine
> he taught our hearts to rise;
> 'Tis uncorrupted, undefil'd,
> unfading in the skies.
>
> Saints by the pow'r of God are kept
> till the salvation come:
> We walk by faith as strangers here;
> but Christ shall call us home.

Several times a day I committed the dear lady to the Lord and she squeezed my hand in Amen. When all the indignities of dying were over and her family and friends met for her funeral on a gloriously sunny summer day, we sang that hymn and I thought of her safe home in heaven in possession of her divine inheritance and was comforted. Our ends have still to come, and we don't know whether sooner or later, which is why we need to keep short accounts with God and commit our spirits in prayer to him each new day and every night. We were well taught if our childhood prayer was, 'This night as I lie down to sleep, I pray thee, Lord, my soul to keep. If I should die before I wake, I pray thee, Lord, my soul to take.'

8

Copy = Jesus' compassion for the sick and disabled

When we bought our first word processor (how long ago that seems!) one of the functions I found most useful was 'copy and paste'. I was working on my first book at the time and often decided after writing a passage that it would be better placed elsewhere. The decision was made simply enough, the time consuming bit was retyping it. Suddenly it was different. I could copy and paste to my heart's content. Such freedom of choice was almost dizzying! I don't suppose I'm the only Christian who wishes such copying and pasting was possible in the Christian life. How I would love to learn all about Jesus' compassion and then copy and paste it into my own life – altogether and all at once. Life's not like that. Our copying of Jesus is a day by day business, an hour by hour effort.

Jesus had compassion on those who were sick and disabled. We see that in his dealings with two blind men. 'As Jesus and his disciples were leaving Jericho, a large crowd followed him. Two blind men were sitting by the roadside, and when they heard that Jesus was going by, they shouted, "Lord, Son of David, have mercy on us!" The crowd rebuked them and told them to be quiet, but they shouted all the louder, "Lord, Son of David, have mercy on us!" Jesus stopped and called them. "What do you want me to do for you?" he asked. "Lord," they answered, "we want our sight." Jesus had compassion on them and touched their eyes. Immediately they received their sight and followed him' (Matt. 20:29-34).

We would be less than human if seeing those who are ill or disabled did not move our hearts. That is pity. We would be more Christlike if we had compassion rather than pity. Pity feels and compassion does. We can't heal those who are blind or give hearing to those who are deaf. It is not in our power to work miracles; they belong to Jesus. But compassion can work wonders. I am disabled, having been unable to walk without the use of crutches since my mid thirties, over twenty years ago. And I have had wonders worked in my heart by compassionate Christian people – and compassionate friends of no faith at all.

Alastair was my minister when I suddenly found myself in more pain than I could bear. After weeks in hospital I felt shut in our home as I was for a time confined to a wheelchair. Although I had walked with the aid of a calliper for some time before that, it hadn't occurred to me that I was disabled till then. While I was housebound I didn't particularly miss shopping; retail therapy has never felt therapeutic. But I missed attending church more than I can say. I knew I wasn't fit to sit through a service but I felt starved of the Word of God. My concentration was affected by the pain-relieving medication I was taking at the time and my quiet times and listening to sermons on cassette just didn't seem to reach that hungry part of me. Alastair recognised that I was not only disabled but I was starving. He couldn't relieve my pain or take away my disability but he could feed me. On visit after visit after visit he gave me the outline of the previous Sunday morning's sermon and it fed my soul. Angus had already done that on returning home from church, but somehow my distress on Sundays put a barrier between me and what was being held out to me. By the middle of the week, when Alastair came, I was more able to cope.

Sheana became my legs. Recently retired from work, she used her car to take me wherever I needed to go – and with such unobtrusive compassion that I didn't feel guilty about it. She packed my wheelchair in the back of her car and we set off to hospital appointments, meetings, shopping and visiting. I smile when I remember my good friend who is now home with Jesus. She had been brought up in the era of 'the devil finds work for idle hands' and her hands didn't know how to be idle. Sheana was the only person I know who, when she didn't have someone in the passenger seat of her car, kept knitting lying there to pick up and do when she was waiting at red traffic lights! I don't suppose there's a law against knitting when waiting at traffic lights, but perhaps there should be! How she did it I really don't know, but my friend made me feel that I was doing her a favour by taking up so much of her time and energy.

Anne's compassion brought an altogether different gift. Our husbands were both studying for the ministry at the time and Anne worked near our home. Once a week or more she came in to see me before heading for home. Unfortunately Anne has suffered for years from a very painful condition in her back. The precious times we spent together made me refocus – made me look away from the pain that threatened to consume my mind and look at someone else who hurt. She brought the compassion that sprung from her own understanding of pain and taught me that one day ... one day ... my pain might become a tool to help others.

> He cannot heal who has not suffered much,
> For only sorrow, sorrow understands.
> They will not come for healing at our touch
> Who have not seen the scars upon our hands.
>
> (Edwin McNeil Poteat)

Then there was Matti, a Finnish friend, who phoned to ask how I was keeping. When I gave the regulation reply, 'I'm fine, thanks,' he followed up his question with words that burned into my heart. 'Irene, please allow me the privilege of helping to bear your burden.' Matti taught me a huge lesson that day. He taught me that compassion is a privilege; that the bearing of another person's burden is a true – if a weighty – privilege. In the nearly twenty years that have elapsed since Matti's phone call I have been privileged over and over again to share people's burdens. I always try to express the fact that they are putting me in a privileged position, because when you are going through the mill you don't feel as if you have a burden, you feel as though you are a burden.

There have been times when my disability has made me feel compassion for those who are able-bodied. Just one example will explain what I mean. Some twelve years or so after losing my ability to walk, I had a visitor, a fit and healthy woman in her late twenties. We'd never met before. She questioned me about why I couldn't walk, digging quite deeply into my personal story. Then she asked a question I'd never been asked. 'Do you miss walking?' Why is it that strangers sometimes feel able to ask questions our best friends would not? I didn't answer directly; I think I was too taken aback. But I questioned my visitor about her own life, and as she told me her story I felt so sorry for her. She was healthy, comfortably well-off and successful in her work. My visitor was a real product of modern life – you know the type of person. They drive everywhere, eat out a lot and feed on pre-packed meals at home, and their entertainment is in the theatre, the cinema or sitting in front of the television. I could not climb a hill – though I have many happy memories of doing so – but she had never climbed a really high hill. I could not cycle – though I enjoy my exercise bike daily – but she had never learned to ride a bicycle as she'd always been driven to school. I could no longer walk on rough ground and enjoy such things as camping holidays – though I well remember smoky tea and not-quite-cooked potato straight from the campfire – and she just laughed at the thought of that being fun. My heart went out to her. When she is unable to be active she'll have no memories of swimming in the cold sea, of her hair blowing in the wind as she cycled downhill, of reading by torchlight in a tent, of climbing ridge after ridge of a Scottish mountain. And I fear she'll find little comfort in the memory of meals in fine restaurants and good films on the television.

After Jesus had healed people suffering from a wide assortment of disabilities, his compassion was still not exhausted. He 'left there [Tyre and Sidon] and went along the Sea of Galilee. Then he went up on a mountainside and sat down. Great crowds came to him, bringing the lame, the blind, the crippled, the mute and many others, and laid them at his feet; and he healed them. The people were amazed when they saw the mute speaking, the crippled made well, the lame walking and the blind seeing. And they praised the God of Israel. Jesus called his disciples to him and said, 'I have compassion for these people; they have already been with me three days and have nothing to eat. I do not want to send them away hungry, or they may collapse on the way' (Matt. 15:29-32).

The Lord had already healed their diseases, now their sheer physical hunger and weariness provoked him to compassion. There were over four thousand men there, as well as women and children, and he provided a picnic to sustain them until they walked to their homes. Matthew records that 'They all ate and were satisfied' (v. 37). In 1984 television screens beamed out news of appalling suffering in Ethiopia. In March that year the Ethiopian government announced that the country could not produce enough food to keep its population fed and that millions were at risk of starvation. Communism had reigned in the country since the overthrow of Emperor Haile Selassie ten years earlier. Western governments feared that money sent as aid would find its way into the Marxist-Leninist coffers. By October the pictures in news reports were so shocking that the UK public donated £5,000,000 in just three days. By December Western countries had sent more than £100,000,000, and the Band Aid single 'Do they know it's Christmas' brought in a further £8,000,000. The dire situation continued to inspire compassion throughout the following year when two Live Aid charity concerts raised millions of pounds. Pictures of emaciated mothers holding infants with swollen empty bellies touched the hearts of millions and compassion led to giving on an unprecedented scale.

Twenty years later such shocking pictures don't seem to shock us quite so much. In 1984 we thought the worst of the problem was confined to Ethiopia, now we know that drought can cause starvation throughout Sub-Saharan Africa. Could it be that the problem has just become too big for us to feel we can do anything about it? Is it that our givings are already committed up to the limit we can afford? Or have we just seen so many pictures of so many emaciated mothers with starving swollen-bellied babies that we don't really take it in anymore, that what would once have provoked generous compassion now only inspires pity that feels sorry for the poor souls and hopes, in a vague way, that governments will do something to help them. I'm afraid that the last of these three options is the truth because when we do see some 'novel' tragedy played out on our television screens we can still be prompted into giving amazing amounts of money. The tsunami that hit the countries surrounding the Indian Ocean on Boxing Day 2004 made that abundantly clear.

Jesus felt compassion for the hungry crowd. We are Jesus' representatives, his co-workers here on earth, and his compassion, felt so long ago in Israel, has not failed today, even if ours has. 'Because of the Lord's great love we are not consumed, for his compassions never fail' (Lam. 3:22). It does us no harm to remember that but for the grace of God we might have been born in Ethiopia in the early 1980s or in Ache in Indonesia at the turn of the new century.

9

Copy = Jesus' compassion for the outcast

Scripture records that Jesus had compassion on the outcast. 'A man with leprosy came to him and begged him on his knees, "If you are willing, you can make me clean." Filled with compassion, Jesus reached out his hand and touched the man. "I am willing," he said. "Be clean!" Immediately the leprosy left him and he was cured' (Mark 1:40-42). From the time his leprosy was diagnosed that man would not have felt the touch of a hand other than that of a fellow-sufferer. Leprosy was thought to be very contagious and children would be still very young when they were warned to stay away from those who suffered from the disease. To facilitate their segregation, those who were leprous had to call out and warn any who were coming close to them that it was unsafe to do so. Men and women who had the condition stayed outside towns and villages. It is no accident that the Lord met this man while 'he travelled throughout Galilee' (v. 39) rather than when he was resident in a specific community.

The man must have heard about Jesus' healing ministry; why else would he have approached him with this huge request? And he came in faith. Note that he doesn't say, 'If you can, please make me clean.' Rather, his request is, 'If you are willing, you can make me clean.' Jesus' compassion made him very willing indeed. Reaching out, he touched the man – before he had healed him from his disease. Only then did he indicate his willingness to heal and take away the leprosy. Those who watched must have been both appalled and confused. If he insisted on touching the man, why didn't he wait until he was healed? After all, it was only a matter of a minute or two. But Jesus' compassion had him touch the outcast, while he was still an outcast, before restoring him to membership of the community. That cannot but bring to mind the fact that the Lord loved us so much that, while we were yet sinners, he died for us.

Mary Verghese was brought up in a privileged family in South India in the 1930s. Many happy memories of her childhood went with her into adult life, but it was a sad memory that haunted her. She was playing in the garden of her home when she heard a piercing cry, 'Praise the Lord! Praise the Lord!' The child ran to the open gate and saw a figure approaching. She thought – only thought – it was a man, moving in an odd stiff sort of a way. 'As he came closer, she saw that both his feet were heavily bandaged. His hands also were wound all about with dirty cloths, and the protruding fingers did not look like fingers at all. They were unshapely stumps. It was his face, however, that looked strangest of all. He had no eyebrows. His skin hung loosely over his cheekbones, and there was a queer flatness where his nose should have been' (from *Take My Hands* by Dorothy Clarke Wilson). Before Mary could get any closer warnings rang out from several directions that the beggar had leprosy and her ayah rushed to drag her away from danger. From then on, despite studying medicine, Mary had a fear of working with people with leprosy.

During her medical training Mary Verghese was involved in a dreadful road accident that left her horribly disfigured and, after a very long period of rehabilitation, only mobile in a wheelchair. Dorothy Clarke Wilson records a conversation that took place while the young medical student was still bed-bound. Dr Paul Brand, who was world famous for the corrective surgery he carried out on the hands of people suffering from leprosy, visited Mary in her room.

'I think it's time, Mary, that you began thinking about your future.'

She smiled wearily. 'Do you suppose I ever think of anything else?'

'I mean your professional future. Your future career as a doctor.'

She stared at him. It was not like Dr Brand to jest about serious matters. 'My ... surely you must be joking.'

'I am certainly not. You don't think your professional life has to be over, do you, just because you'll probably never walk again?'

Mary's heart was pounding. 'But how ...,' she whispered.

'In a few more weeks you'll be sitting in a wheelchair. You still have your arms, good strong ones, and your hands, extremely skilful ones. And your mind ...' His eyes twinkled, 'such as it is.'

With Dr John Brand's encouragement Mary Verghese became involved in the same reconstructive surgery and spent her working life helping those who suffered from the effects of leprosy to live as normally and usefully as they could. I wonder if Mary sometimes compared Jesus' compassionate touch and her initial fear of contact with someone who was leprous. Yet by God's grace, and despite every human probability, the Lord enabled her to work what must have seemed like miracles on her patients.

Jesus calls his people today to have compassion on those who are cast out of our society, and there is an increasing number of them. I don't think I saw a beggar on a Scottish street until the late 1980s. The first time I saw a child begging was in Dublin in 1994. Some have been cast out by drug misuse, others by AIDS and many just because their families have broken up round about them and there is nowhere to call home and nowhere to go. One of my friends, a London City Missionary, worked with homeless people in the Waterloo area of that great city. Unbeknown to him, his expression of compassion for an outcast made a deep impression on a passer-by. The man wrote to London City Mission in the following terms.

I walk past the above premises several times each week. I have become familiar with some of the faces and occasionally exchange greeting with them. That said, once passed by they disappear from your thoughts pretty quick.

However, yesterday morning was rather different. I walked down Webber Street and side stepped one of the regulars who was face down on the ground, semi-conscious with his hand outstretched towards a beer can. People scurried past, often averting their eyes. They do not consider these 'down-and-outs' worthy of any attention or indeed sympathy. Then I noticed a young man descend from the stairs of your mission. Watching, as I had stopped to have a conversation on my mobile phone, I initially assumed he was coming to make this vagrant move on. But no. Instead he crouched beside this forlorn figure and stroked his face with tenderness and apparent affection.

It was a moving and somewhat shameful moment for me. It made me realise that this person on the street was a real person just like me, albeit perhaps less fortunate. I am grateful for that realisation.

I hope that the attached contribution can be used to assist in the good work of the Webber Street mission.

As the writer of that letter chatted on his mobile phone he saw such a tender act of compassion that it prompted him, in his compassion, to write a cheque that would help with Jesus' work among the outcasts of London.

For some years past my husband and I have attended the Keswick Convention for a week each summer. Knowing that there is no way I can retain the content of the number of fine sermons we hear preached, I note just a small thing from each, something that I can apply to my life in the year to come. On one occasion Professor Don Carson, of Trinity Evangelical Divinity School in Deerfield, Illinois, opened God's Word in a most remarkable way. The practical thing I took from one of his sermons was this: that a church should wear as a badge of honour any misfit who comes along to the services. That was a reminder to me to try to see people as Jesus sees them and to feel something of his compassion for them.

Copy – Jesus' compassion for the aimless
The Lord also had compassion on those who were living hassled, aimless lives. 'Jesus went through all the towns and villages, teaching in their synagogues, preaching the good news of the kingdom and healing every disease and sickness. When he saw the crowds, he had compassion on

them, because they were harassed and helpless, like sheep without a shepherd. Then he said to his disciples, "The harvest is plentiful but the workers are few. Ask the Lord of the harvest, therefore, to send out workers into his harvest field"' (Matt. 9:35-38). In the passage it is not disease or sickness that provokes Jesus' compassion; rather it is the fact that the people are harassed and helpless. It is so much easier to feel compassion for the sick, the disabled, even perhaps the outcast, than it is for the vast majority of people who are spiritually aimless and perpetually hassled by life. That is so much the norm that we don't often see the terrible seriousness of the situation.

Jesus is the Good Shepherd. He recognises that these people are like sheep without a shepherd; sinners without the Good Shepherd, therefore without hope, hopeless. No wonder his heart went out to them. There is perhaps no area in which I (and perhaps you) need to be more prayerful than this, that I might recognise what a truly awful position it is to be without Christ and without hope in the world or for eternity. It boils down to the fact that I need to take God at his word and his Word more seriously.

The facts I need to remember are these.

Not one single human being is naturally good or acceptable to God. 'There is no one righteous, not even one; there is no one who understands, no one who seeks God. All have turned away, they have together become worthless; there is no-one who does good, not even one' (Rom. 3:10-12).

Jesus Christ is the one and only way to God. Jesus said, 'I am the way and the truth and the life. No one comes to the Father except through me' (John 14:6).

Our response to Jesus determines our eternal destiny. Jesus said, 'I tell you, whoever acknowledges me before men, the Son of Man will also acknowledge him before the angels of God. But he who disowns me before men will be disowned before the angels of God' (Luke 12:8-9).

There is free and full forgiveness for those who repent and come to Christ. 'If we confess our sins, he is faithful and just and will forgive us our sins and purify us from all unrighteousness' (1 John 1:9).

Those who do not come to Christ in repentance and faith are condemned. Jesus said, 'For God so loved the world that he gave his one and only Son, that whoever believes in him shall not perish but have eternal life. … Whoever believes in him is not condemned, but whoever does not believe stands condemned already because he has not believed in the name of God's one and only Son' (John 3:16, 18).

Those who don't know Jesus need to be told about his offer of salvation. 'How, then, can they call on the one they have not believed in? And how can they believe in the one of whom they have not heard? And how can they hear without someone preaching to them? And how can they preach unless they are sent? As it is written, "How beautiful are the feet of those who bring good news"' (Rom. 10:14-15).

No wonder the Lord's reaction to seeing the harassed and helpless crowd was to say to his disciples, 'The harvest is plentiful but the workers are few. Ask the Lord of the harvest, therefore, to send out workers into his harvest field' (Matt. 9:37-38). And that leaves me with three questions. Is my response to the sorry plight of the godless to pray to the Lord to send his people to tell them the gospel? Even if I do that, might I be the one God has chosen to pass on the good news to some of those I know? And am I doing that, or am I watching without comment as they move towards a godless eternity? Compassion is strong stuff.

10

Copy = Jesus' humility

This whole book could be about the one computer command – copy. And many books have been written on the subject of copying Jesus. That should be, after all, the heart's desire and aim of every Christian. But for the purposes of this book I just want to mention one other area in which we seek to copy Jesus, that is, in his humility.

When I was a teenaged Christian someone older and wiser told me that the proud think they are humble and the truly humble feel condemned by their pride. Even in my teens I could see that this was true. I was one of a group of young believers and we cooked up some very strange theology between us. One of our set was of the opinion that his sins were forgiven and he was therefore sinless. I think that can be called the 'simple in the extreme' branch of theology, most often held by young people who haven't yet emerged into the real world. The sad thing was that my friend was proud of his supposed sinlessness.

Another of that little company was a much more sensitive individual who knew herself a little better. Since becoming a Christian she was concerned about her godless pride. Those of us who knew her well recognised her as a sweet and humble person who saw her pride only because she compared herself, quite rightly, with Jesus rather than with the rest of us. And as the years have gone by I have met others like her, most of them elderly Christians ripening for heaven who see their sin of pride ever more clearly as they draw nearer and nearer to their Lord. One of the privileges of being in a small congregation in which there are a number of elderly people is seeing the beauty of Jesus reflected in them as their focus turns from earth to heaven.

Humility should characterise our lives. After all, as Christians we know we are nothing that God did not make us and we can do nothing worthwhile unless he enables us. But what has humility to do with Jesus, the Lord of glory? 'Do nothing out of selfish ambition or vain conceit, but in humility consider others better than yourselves. Each of you should look not only to your own interests, but also to the interests of others. Your attitude should be the same as that of Christ Jesus: Who, being in very nature God, did not consider equality with God something to be grasped, but made himself nothing, taking the very nature of a servant, being made in human likeness. And being found in appearance as a man, he humbled himself and became obedient to death – even death on a cross!' (Phil. 2:3-8).

It is certainly true of Christ that he did nothing out of selfish ambition or vain conceit. In the councils of eternity he agreed to exchange the glories of heaven for a time here on earth. Nor did he choose a life of earthly luxury and ease. Jesus was born in the lowliest of circumstances (Luke 2:7). His family became refugees shortly after his birth (Matt. 2:13-17). He earned his living doing manual work (Mark 6:3). For the three years of his itinerant ministry he had no settled home (Matt. 8:20). His own brothers did not believe in him (John 7:5). In fact, his family was so concerned that 'they went to take charge of him, for they said, "He is out of his mind"' (Mark 3:21). Unable to prove Jesus guilty of any crime (Luke 23:4), Pilate handed him over to be crucified in order to satisfy a rabble (Mark 15:15). Jesus was crucified for no sin of his own and buried in a borrowed tomb (Matt. 27:59-60). All that is true of the King of Creation, the one in whom, and by whom, all things are made and sustained. What humility!

Christ's humility was borne of obedience. The fruit of his obedience – even to death on the cross – was the salvation for all eternity of those who were chosen before the beginning of time. Our hope of heaven is the fruit of Christ's obedience. How hard won it was, and how humbly grateful that should make us.

In what ways can we copy Jesus in his humility? The Bible gives us some answers to that question. We should avoid doing things out of selfish ambition or vain conceit. If we preach or teach, it should never be said of us that we enjoy the sound of our own voice. The job of the preacher and teacher is to point away from himself to the crucified Saviour. But preachers are not the only ones subject to Satan's wiles. It is so easy to accept glory rather than giving it to Christ. From my own experience as a Christian writer I know this to be true. When someone tells me that one of my books has been helpful, Satan immediately jumps to attention and dangles the temptation to be proud. I have to remember that my books are written 'as to the Lord' not in some kind of ego trip. I may feel thankful when something I write speaks to the heart of a reader, but thankfulness and pride are poles apart.

Johann Sebastian Bach, a Christian and one of the greatest composers of all time, wrote on his compositions, 'To the glory of God.' When he heard his organ pieces played magnificently he wanted the Lord to be glorified rather than himself. Frances Ridley Havergal, one of England's most prolific hymn-writers, wished none of the praise for what she wrote. The last verse of her well-known hymn 'Take my life, and let it be consecrated, Lord, to thee,' expressed her humility beautifully.

> Take my will, and make it thine;
> It shall be no longer mine.
> Take my heart – it is thine own;
> It shall be thy royal throne.
> Take my love; my Lord, I pour
> At thy feet its treasure-store.
> Take myself, and I will be
> Ever, only, all for thee.

How different was Frances's sentiment to how that hymn often sounds when it is announced. 'Take my life, and let it be,' suggests that we are giving our lives to the Lord then taking them right back again. Thankfully there are some preachers who remember to 'let it be consecrated'!

Then we are told to 'in humility consider others better' than ourselves. Note, in humility rather than in pretence. I think the secret of doing this is to be found in the old believers of whom I wrote earlier. As they ripen for glory they look less in the direction of earth and more in the direction of heaven. And when they view themselves in the light of Jesus they see the truth of scripture's statement that even our good deeds are as filthy rags (Isa. 64:6). Perhaps when we are tempted towards feelings of superiority we should look away from the person who makes us feel 'good' and look to Jesus, in the brilliance of whose glory we will see just a little of what we really are.

If we strive to copy Jesus' humility we will look not only to our own interests, but also to the interests of others (Phil. 2:4). We live in an amazingly egocentric age. The very first children's talk I can remember hearing in church was on the subject of JOY. Our minister took the three letters of the word and explained that we could only have true joy if we put the letters of the word in the right order. J came first, and Jesus should come first in our lives. O came next, and others come after Jesus. Y, for yourself, came last of all. That was only fifty years ago, but it would not go down well today where I come first, mine come second, others fit in if and when there is space, and Jesus is most often left out altogether.

Jesus lived to humbly do the will of his Father. Even as a boy of twelve or thirteen, when he became separated from his parents, he was surprised that they didn't know they would find him in the temple. "'Why were you searching for me?" he asked. "Didn't you know I had to be in my Father's house?'" (Luke 2:49). Years later, when his disciples were discussing food, the Lord used the opportunity to show them how important it was to him to do God's will. "'My food,' said Jesus, "is to do the will of him who sent me and to finish his work'" (John 4:34). Doing his Father's will *was* Jesus' life. Is our priority first and foremost not to look to our own interest, but to the interest and will of God? Then is it our priority to serve others?

Jesus said, "'Love the Lord your God with all your heart and with all your soul and with all your mind.' This is the first and greatest commandment. And the second is like it: "Love your neighbour as yourself." All the Law and the Prophets hang on these two commandments' (Matt. 22:37-40). Humility, loving and serving cannot be separated. The newly married couple delight in doing little things for each other. The parents of a tiny baby perform even the messiest of jobs with deep affection. The degree to which we truly love others can be measured in how we humbly serve them.

When I became a Christian at sixteen years of age I already went to church, though I was not brought up in a family that set much store by attendance at public worship. I remember my minister with such warmth and affection. One day I asked him how Christians were meant to love their neighbours, for I really didn't understand how I could love people I hardly knew. He explained that love was not just a feeling, it was also a doing, and that as I humbly served people I would grow to love them. A week or two later he asked me to remain behind after Bible Class, and when I did he gave me the names of two elderly and housebound ladies. 'Serve them humbly and you'll discover that you love them.' I visited one of them weekly until she died and the other until I married and left the area. My minister knew what he was doing and I began to learn the lesson he sought to teach me.

Jesus Christ was humbly obedient to his Father's will right to the humiliation of Calvary. Jean Nicolas Grou, a nineteenth-century Jesuit priest, gives a serious reminder of the relationship between humility and humiliation. 'Many who pray for humility would be extremely sorry if God were to grant it to them. … They forget that to love, desire, and ask for humility is loving, desiring and asking for humiliations, for these are the companions … of humility, and without them it is no more than a beautiful but meaningless idea.' After Christ's final humiliation came glory! 'Therefore God exalted him to the highest place and gave him the name that is above every name, that at the name of Jesus every knee should bow, in heaven and on earth and under the earth, and every tongue confess that Jesus Christ is Lord, to the glory of God the Father' (Phil. 2:9-11). And there is glory at the end for God's people too, eternity spent in the glorious company of the Saviour.

11

THE RULER AND TOOLS

Recently I acquired a new computer. It has a larger than normal screen to facilitate my layout work on *The Instructor* magazine. Unfortunately some of what was on toolbars on my previous computer is along the side of the screen on this one, and in very small print. I asked our local computer expert if he could find a way of increasing their size, but after turning his head at right-angles to the world, and sitting uncomfortably close to the screen for several thoughtful minutes, he had to admit defeat. I'll just need to learn what the tools are and remember them.

Thankfully God is infinitely more helpful. Having made the world and human society, he gave ten rules which, if kept, would facilitate the smooth running of humankind. Unfortunately the warp that entered human nature at the Fall prevents us from keeping God's rules, and it is our inability to keep them that changes them into tools. God uses the Ten Commandments as tools to teach us our need of repentance and forgiveness. They are the ruler against which our rightness – our righteousness – is measured. Each time we move away from the straightness of the ruler by breaking one of his laws we bring God's judgement on ourselves. 'Whoever keeps the whole law and yet stumbles at just one point is guilty of breaking all of it' (James 2:10). Only through the death of Jesus at Calvary can we avoid his final condemnation.

Even as we read through the Ten Commandments we are convicted of our failure to keep them. The Lord uses them like a surgeon's scalpel to show us our need of radical surgery for the removal of sin and guilt. Some argue that the Commandments have been superseded by the teaching of Jesus, when he answered the question, 'Which is the greatest commandment in the Law?' 'Jesus replied: "Love the Lord your God with all your heart and with all your soul and with all your mind." This is the first and greatest commandment. And the second is like it: "Love your neighbour as yourself." All the Law and Prophets hang on these two commandments' (Matt. 22:36-40).

Did the Lord remove eight of the Ten Commandments and just leave us with two to be getting on with? Was eighty percent of what his Father had given to Moses obsolete? Absolutely not. The first four of the Ten Commandments are encapsulated in 'Love the Lord your God with all your heart and with all your soul and with all your mind.' If we truly love the Lord, we will not want to have other gods before him. Nor will we wish to make idols in any shape or form and worship them. We certainly won't use his name as a swear word or intentionally defile his holy day. The remaining six Commandments are encapsulated in loving our neighbour as ourselves. If we love our parents, we will honour them. And if we truly love others we will not murder them, commit adultery with them or against them, steal from them, lie to them or about them, or have a covetous desire for what they possess. Jesus did not negate God's Commandments, rather he summed them up in answer to a trick question. Matthew records, 'Hearing that Jesus had silenced the Sadducees, the Pharisees got together. One of them, an expert in the law, tested him with this question, "Teacher, which is the greatest commandment in the Law?"' (Matt. 22:34-36). The Lord brilliantly cut a swathe through the morass of laws that the Jewish theologians had added to God's Ten Commandments and then summarised all ten in two: love God and love others as you love yourself. 'What is the greatest commandment?' the Pharisee asked. And Jesus replied – the ones God gave you.

When I was teaching my Sunday School children the story of God giving the Ten Commandments to Moses, I told them about the supernatural events that surrounded that occasion. 'Mount Sinai was covered with smoke, because the Lord descended on it in fire. The smoke billowed up from it like smoke from a furnace, the whole mountain trembled violently, and the sound of the trumpet grew louder and louder. Then Moses spoke and the voice of God answered him' (Exod. 19:18-19). I asked the children why they thought all these things happened. One boy had a splendid answer. 'The earth was covered with smoke and shook when the Lord came down because it was so excited.' Out of the mouths of babes ...

God's rules become tools when they turn us to him in repentance. On 18th November 1834, a young Scots minister wrote a hymn that was in fact his testimony. It is called 'Jehovah Tsidkenu' – the Lord our Righteousness. The hymn traces his journey through carelessness to a sentimental approach to Christianity, through an encounter with God's Law when grace opened his eyes (then legal fears shook me, I trembled to die) to his coming to saving faith in Jesus. The young minister was Robert Murray McCheyne, whose beautiful Christ-likeness was recognised in his own day, and whose early death lent a pathos to his story. What he wrote perfectly illustrates God's rules being used as God's tools.

I once was a stranger to grace and to God,
I knew not my danger; and felt not my load;
Though friends spoke in rapture of Christ on the tree,
Jehovah Tsidkenu was nothing to me.

I oft read with pleasure, to soothe or engage,
Isaiah's wild measure and John's simple page;
But e'en when they pictured the blood-sprinkled tree,
Jehovah Tsidkenu seemed nothing to me.

Like tears from the daughters of Zion that roll,
I wept when the waters went over his soul,
Yet thought not that my sins had nailed to the tree
Jehovah Tsidkenu – 'twas nothing to me.

When free grace awoke me by light from on high,
Then legal fears shook me, I trembled to die;
No refuge, no safety in self could I see –
Jehovah Tsidkenu my Saviour must be.

My terrors all vanished before the sweet name;
My guilty fear banished, with boldness I came
To drink at the fountain, life-giving and free –
Jehovah Tsidkenu is all things to me.

Jehovah Tsidkenu! My treasure and boast,
Jehovah Tsidkenu! I ne'er can be lost;
In thee shall I conquer by flood and by field –
My cable, my anchor, my breastplate and shield!

Even treading the valley; the shadow of death,
This 'watchword' shall rally my faltering breath;
For while from life's fever my God sets me free,
Jehovah Tsidkenu my death-song shall be.

12

THE WORSHIPPING GOD TOOLBAR

God said, 'I am the LORD your God, who brought you out of Egypt, out of the land of slavery. You shall have no other gods before me' (Exod. 20:2-3). God begins by reminding his people who he is and what he has done for them in the past. You would think they would need no reminding. After all, it's not every day that a sea opens up to let you through and then crashes back down on the enemy army that's pursuing you in order to reclaim you as slaves. But time had passed since their great deliverance and God seemed to be delaying entry to the promised land. Not only that, the journey had brought them into contact with pagan tribes who had interesting looking gods, idols made of silver and gold. And all they had was a concept of God, nothing tangible at all.

The Free Church of Scotland, to which I belong, has a programme of Easter and summer camps. This year over four hundred young people are going to camp. These camps have been singularly blessed in recent years, with many young people coming home changed having met with Jesus. Some of them go back to non-Christian homes and churches where there are no other young people. And it can be a struggle. At first they go on in the afterglow of camp. Then there is the camp reunion to look forward to in November. After that winter sets in, sometimes a winter of the soul as well as the season of the year. They may have no Christian friends in school and no believing teachers to support them. Perhaps they see their contemporaries exploring things that begin to look attractive: alcohol, soft drugs, sex. And they wonder what harm is in them. After all, God made everything; surely we should enjoy what we can, when we can. The Lord may use serious and painful tools to bring his infant child back to his rule: 'I am the Lord your God, who brought you out of Egypt, out of the land of slavery. You shall have no other gods before me.'

I was not brought up in a Christian home, but in my teen years I was blessed to have a believing teacher. There was a small Scripture Union group in school which he attended when he could. His quiet support and encouragement helped me to grow, and his obvious deep love of God's Word encouraged me to read the new translation of the Bible he gave me. It was a great thrill just a few years ago to meet him again and to have the opportunity to thank him for what he had done for me all those years ago. Older Christians should never underestimate the impression they can make on a young person's life. I probably learned more from watching my teacher day by day in the classroom than I did from listening to him at Scripture Union as I had few Christian role models.

Throughout our Christian lives we need to hold on to God's first rule as a tool to keep us thankful and worshipping him alone. I have a friend who reviews her life monthly. She has a list of questions she asks herself month after month and, depending on how she is able to answer them, she makes changes to the devotional and practical aspects of her life. Some years ago I attended a doctor for pain relief and over time we became friends. We spoke at some meetings together and did a little writing work too. Living on opposite sides of the county, we only saw each other once a year or so after I stopped being his patient. I found our meetings really helpful as they made me look back and review what had happened since the last time we met and how I had coped. It was especially helpful in relation to my pain as I realised over time that although it was always there, I was finding new ways of living with it. Looking back over the past can be most instructive.

The first commandment encourages us to note past deliverances. 'I am the Lord your God, who brought you out of Egypt, out of the land of slavery.' In one of the loveliest psalms in the Bible, David is engaged in a review of past deliverances. 'I waited patiently for the Lord; he turned to me and heard my cry. He lifted me out of the slimy pit, out of the mud and mire; he set my feet on a rock and gave me a firm place to stand. He put a new song in my mouth, a hymn of praise to our God. Many will see and fear and put their trust in the Lord' (Ps. 40:1-3). And the memory reminds him of the uselessness of other so-called gods. 'Blessed is the man who makes the Lord his trust, who does not look to the proud, to those who turn aside to false gods (v. 4). Thinking on these things sends David into a rapture of worship. 'Many, O Lord my God, are the wonders you have done. The things you planned for us no-one can recount to you; were I to speak and tell of them, they would be too many to declare' (v. 5).

When we review past deliverances we recognise that only God the Lord can deliver and, therefore, only he is worthy of our worship. Of course, the final and most wonderful expression of God's deliverance is our salvation through his Son, Jesus Christ. If we read that into the deliverance referred to in the first commandment, how can we acknowledge any other god, how can we worship anyone but Jesus? Our Egypt is this sin-warped world. In our land of slavery we are held captive by Satan and captivated by sin. Like David, Christians should rejoice in wonder when they read the words of the Law. 'I am the Lord your God, who brought you out of Egypt, out of the land of slavery. You shall have no other gods before me.' Using the first Commandment as a tool, we can make a practice of reviewing our deliverances, especially our deliverance from condemnation and hell, and so encourage our wandering eyes away from the other well-disguised gods that Satan dangles in front of us.

13

The
AVOIDING IDOLATRY
TOOLBAR

God says, 'You shall not make for yourself an idol in the form of anything in heaven above or on the earth beneath or in the waters below. You shall not bow down to them or worship them; for I, the LORD your God, am a jealous God, punishing the children for the sin of the fathers to the third and fourth generation of those who hate me, but showing love to a thousand generations of those who love me and keep my commandments' (Exod. 20:4-6). God's rule is clear beyond any contradiction – he will allow no idol worship, and the penalties against it are severe.

Breaking the commandment into its parts shows us that idols are man made, even when they are representations of something or someone heavenly. They are produced for the purpose of worship. God detests idols because worship is due to him and him alone, and his punishment for their use extends down the generations, as does the blessing that follows right worship and the keeping of his commandments. How can we use these facts as tools to help us keep our worship holy and pleasing to the Lord our God?

On the face of it idols are easily identified. We see them as statues and shrines, totems, charms and other such things that feel quite foreign to believers. But do we stop to consider the 'acceptable' idols of today, things like security, success and recognition? Is our work done 'as to the Lord' or as to the bank balance or the garden centre, designer labels or the car, the house or the latest hi-tech electronic gizmo? Considering how seriously God looks on idolatry we take it in a fearfully light way, especially as we know without a shadow of doubt that our aspirations (which Satan delights in turning into idols) do carry on through generations to come. Our 'having arrived' often becomes the next generation's starting point, and so it goes on.

In my early childhood our living room had varnished wooden floors with rugs on them, some of them rag-rugs made by my grandmother. Then my parents saved up for a carpet square that was really a large rug that covered most of the centre of the room. By the time I was in my late teens fitted carpets were the latest 'must have', and my mother saved for a very long time to fit our home with carpets. In fact, she cheated, buying instead strips of carpeting and sewing them to the shape and size of each room – and what a marathon effort that was. When Angus and I married in 1971 and set up our first home, Mum was disappointed that we started off with a carpet square on a varnished wooden floor. She had hoped for better for us and saw that in terms of her 'having struggled to get there' being our starting point. How she would have shaken her head today as people dispose of their fitted carpets, sand and varnish the wooden floorboards underneath, then look for rugs to suit the new trendy décor!

The devil must be delighted when he can tempt us to turn heavenly things into idols. It goes without saying that worshipping an image of the Lord is anathema. Would we worship a statue of our child or a photograph of our husband or wife? So what heavenly things can become idols? Heaven offers eternal security for God's people, but do we long for – and make an idol of – security on earth? Heaven offers everlasting peace to God's people, but do we sometimes accept peace at any price, thus making an idol of it? Heaven offers joy in the nearer presence of Jesus, but do we ever make enjoyment our idol and use whether or not we enjoy things as the basis of many of our choices? There will be no pain or illness or death in heaven, but have we turned good health and continuing youth into an idol when we spend more money on our gym membership, 'health' foods, vitamin and mineral supplements and the latest running shoes than we offer to the Lord? God says, 'You shall not make for yourself an idol in the form of anything in heaven above ...'

Or ' ... in the earth beneath or in the waters below. You shall not bow down and worship them ...' In this Commandment God gives us a tool to help us evaluate our relationship with his creation. Having created Adam and Eve, 'God blessed them and said to them, "Be fruitful and increase in number; fill the earth and subdue it. Rule over the fish of the sea and the birds of the air and over every living creature that moves on the ground"' (Gen. 1:28). What a mess we have made of our stewardship! Some mine for silver and form it into the shape of a Buddha and worship it, others turn it into exquisite jewellery and – thinking themselves much more sophisticated than the Buddhist – worship that instead. Some believe that God is in all parts of creation and worship tree spirits. Others begin from the same premise and argue the case for the equality of plants, animals and people. We are called to be stewards of creation, which implies keeping it in the Creator's name for generations to come, not raping in a lust for greed. We are not called to worship anything that God has made, whether in its basic elementary form or in whatever way man has made it. Gold – whether statues or Olympic medals – can both become idols. Human beings – individual or mankind, footballer, Nobel Prize winner or film star – all are created, and their greatness is in how much they reflect the image of their Creator. We really do need to take a long hard look at what means most to us then consider whether it is created or Creator. Or in the terms of Exodus chapter 20, we need to take a long hard look at what means most to us then consider what or who we worship.

It would be more comfortable to think about these things if God had stopped the commandment there and left us to think it through. But he did not. He reinforces what he commands by saying that we must worship no one and nothing but him because he is a jealous God. Jealousy is a demand for the rights of exclusive ownership, and we have all seen unpleasant examples of jealousy in action. Think of the film star pipped at the post for an Oscar. You can almost feel her firing poison darts through her smile as someone with a minor role in her film is presented with an award. It is *her* film! Vast sums of money have been spent on court cases that contest the ownership of ideas. Is Dan Brown's *The Da Vinci Code* original, or did it owe its origins to Michael Baigent and Richard Leigh's *Holy Blood; Holy Grail*? It certainly owes no more than a passing nod to the real Jesus. Brown jealously defended that the idea was *his*, Baigent and Leigh contested that it was *theirs*. Jealousy results from feeling that what you are owed, through ownership, is not being given to you. God says: I made you; I made everything. There is nothing that you can see, touch, taste, hear or smell that I did not make. Therefore I am due your worship, your exclusive worship. And I will punish anyone who worships anything or anyone that I have made instead of me, and that punishment will go from generation to generation. We cannot say that we have not been warned.

14

GOD'S NAME AND HIS RULES FOR ITS USE

God says, 'You shall not misuse the name of the LORD your God, for the LORD will not hold anyone guiltless who misuses his name' (Exod. 20:7). The third commandment follows from the second in that God owns his name, he owns it exclusively, and he will not have it either used wrongly or used of another. To call anything a god is to steal from God, who alone is God. To use the word god with a small 'g' is meaningless. There is only one God and he is God the Lord. He has absolute exclusive rights to the title. Where god with a small 'g' is used, idol is intended.

Over the course of history, Jewish people began to invoke God's name as part of an oath. Like the child who backs up a promise with 'cross my heart', the practice probably started with something fairly innocuous. As the years passed generation after generation would have to use more and more sacred objects as the backing for their promises in order to 'top' what had gone before, until they were treading on very dangerous ground indeed. The Lord says, 'I will stretch out my hand against Judah and against all who live in Jerusalem. I will cut off from this place ... those who bow down on the housetops to worship the starry host, those who bow down and swear by the LORD and who also swear by Molech, those who turn back from following the LORD and neither seek the LORD nor enquire of him' (Zeph. 1:4-6). Using the Lord's name as an oath is right in there with worshipping stars and the heathen idol Molech!

It is not difficult to catch Jesus' frustration and anger on the subject of using his holy things as reinforcement on an oath. 'Woe to you, blind guides! You say, "If anyone swears by the temple, it means nothing; but if anyone swears by the gold of the temple, he is bound by his oath." You blind fools! Which is greater: the gold, or the temple that makes the gold sacred? You also say, "If anyone swears by the altar, it means nothing; but if anyone swears by the gift on it, he is bound by his oath." You blind men! Which is greater: the gift, or the altar that makes the gift sacred? Therefore, he who swears by the altar swears by it and by everything on it. And he who swears by the temple swears by it and by the one who dwells in it. And he who swears by heaven swears by God's throne and by the one who sits on it' (Matt. 23:16-22). And the Lord says elsewhere, 'I tell you, Do not swear at all: either by heaven, for it is God's throne; or by the earth, for it is his footstool; or by Jerusalem, for it is the city of the Great King. And do not swear by your head, for you cannot make even one hair white or black. Simply let your "Yes" be "Yes", and your "No", "No"; anything beyond this comes from the evil one' (Matt. 5:34-37).

How can we use this most sombre and serious rule as a tool in our Christian living? It should not even need to be stated that believers never use God's name in vain. But perhaps it does need to be stated that we should wage war against his name being taken in vain by other people. In this politically correct age in which we live, if the name of Allah were used as an oath in the media, the Muslim population would be up in arms and it would hit the headlines on the next news broadcast and the front pages of the newspapers. How feeble we are at complaining when God's name is used in vain. Or are we so inured to it that we don't even actually hear it? Does the frequent misuse of God's holy name melt into the verbal wallpaper with which we are constantly surrounded?

The Commandment tells us that 'the Lord will not hold anyone guiltless who misuses his name.' Is it going too far to say, by extension, that they are also guilty who hear God's name misused and do nothing to prevent it happening again? A year or two ago I met a friend I'd not seen for a very long time. It was great to see him. The only thing that troubled me was that he used the Lord's name as a swear word, or that's what it sounded like. In fact, it was actually being used as a kind of comma. Eventually I explained that I love the Lord Jesus Christ with all my heart and it really hurts me to hear his name being used in this way. My friend no longer does that, at least when we speak to each other on the phone. But what a cop-out! I asked my friend not to splatter his conversation with God's name because it offended me, not because 'the Lord will not hold him guiltless who misuses his name'! And the awful thing is that I felt I'd done the right thing and was delighted with the result. How often I need to look behind what I say and do to examine my motives. They don't always turn out to be as worthy as they seem.

In the third Commandment God gives us a tool to use not only personally but in our increasingly godless society. Jesus tells his followers that we are the salt of the earth and the light of the world and exhorts us to 'let your light shine before men, that they may see your good deeds and praise your Father in heaven' (Matt. 5:13-16). Perhaps if enough Christians did take a public stand on the third Commandment we might see a change in the media. And, in a strange way, doing so could win believers a little more respect from their Muslim friends who must be thoroughly confused over our apparent willingness to allow God's name to be constantly compromised.

15

RULES AND TOOLS FOR SUNDAYS

God says, 'Remember the Sabbath day by keeping it holy. Six days you shall labour and do all your work, but the seventh day is a Sabbath to the LORD your God. On it you shall not do any work, neither you, nor your son or daughter, nor your manservant or maidservant, nor your animals, nor the alien within your gates. For in six days the LORD made the heavens and the earth, the sea, and all that is in them, but he rested on the seventh day. Therefore the LORD blessed the Sabbath day and made it holy' (Exod. 20:8-11).

When God instituted the Sabbath it was the last day of the week, the day after the completion of his act of creation, the day after he had looked at all he had made and saw it was very good. We must not think that God was exhausted after a strenuous week and ready for a rest; the Creator of all things does not tire like mere mortals! One of the ways in which we bear the image of God is that we are capable of making things, albeit using as tools those things that the Lord has already created. I enjoy being creative, whether in taking a photograph, painting a picture, baking a cake or making a birthday card for a friend. Often when I complete a project I leave the finished article where I can see it and then keep going back to look at it. It's a nice feeling to look at something you have made. I am sure that God greatly enjoyed that first of all Sabbaths as he rested and delighted in his creation. It is interesting to note that the ordinance of the Sabbath was instituted before the Fall. Mankind was to observe a weekly Sabbath while thorns and thistles still knew their place and before caring for Creation became burdensome toil.

When Jesus' disciples were accused of Sabbath-breaking by eating ears of corn they picked as they walked along, the Lord told their accusers, 'The Sabbath was made for man, not man for the Sabbath. So the Son of Man is Lord even of the Sabbath' (Mark 2:27-28). God knew man's need for a Sabbath, a day of rest, a weekly day of re-creation, and provided for his need. Not only that, but dependents, those who could be overworked or exploited, whether man or animal, were provided for as well, right down to the visiting stranger and the cow in the field.

After the Lord's resurrection, the first day became the Sabbath rather than the seventh, a weekly reminder of the risen Christ and the empty tomb. We think of Russia being a Communist rather than a Christian country, and so it was for most of last century. Before 1917, however, much Russian thinking was influenced by the Christian faith. For example, think of the names we, in the English-speaking world, have given to the days of the week. Sunday derives its name from a sun god. Monday is called after a moon god. Thursday got its name from Thor, the Norse god of war. In the Russian language the day we call Sunday is *Voskresenie*, which means 'the day of resurrection'. Even the Communists didn't change the name of the day. So each time Lenin and Stalin used the Russian word for Sunday they referred to the day of the resurrection of the Lord Jesus Christ! Ironical, isn't it? Those who named Sunday *Voskresenie* did so because they saw every single Sunday as a celebration of the rising of Christ on the first Easter day.

God in his goodness has provided us with a weekly Sabbath and commanded that we keep it holy, separate, apart and different. The commandment becomes a tool when we try to work out how best to make use of this special day, both for ourselves and for those for whom we are responsible. Now, for those in full-time ministry, the concept of a 'restful' Sabbath may need to keep until retirement, for Sundays can be busy days. We leave home just after 10 am for the short run into Tarbert where Angus takes our morning service and I teach Sunday School. Immediately after the service we drive to Campbeltown, fifty minutes away. Circumstances there mean that Angus has to prepare the hall for the service when we arrive and I do some taxiing before the service begins at 12.45. He then takes the service and I teach my second Sunday School. We are both ready for lunch when we have it in the vestry of the Campbeltown church before leaving for the fifty-minute drive home. The evening service in Tarbert, which Angus conducts, is still to come. By the time we arrive home after the service we're tired. My husband can cope with a book on Sunday evenings, but I'm often too tired to concentrate on reading and I just sit quietly and think. And ours is a small congregation, albeit in two places thirty-eight miles apart.

It helps me a great deal to remember that Sunday, God's special day, is a gift for me and to plan ahead to keep it special. Busy as it is, it then becomes a tool that helps me rest awhile, relax and be re-created. Sheba and I take a little longer on our walk on Sunday mornings, whatever the weather. We don't go any further; rather we take it even more slowly than usual and have more frequent stops. There are advantages in walking with a walking frame with a seat! As I've already mentioned, I use my morning walk with the dog as a time of worship, and on Sundays there is rarely a car on the road to disturb my fellowship with God. It's probably my most special thirty minutes of the week. Coming a fairly close second is teaching Sunday School where I deliberately don't use day-school teaching methods, both for the sake of the children and me. The classes are small enough to keep, I hope, an aunt-chatting-with-her-favourite-nephews-and-nieces atmosphere. That's what it feels like to me.

The run to and from Campbeltown is special. I drive in order to give Angus a break between conducting the two services, and I find driving on our country roads both relaxing and pain-relieving. Driving seems to use that part of my brain that feels pain (what does that say about my driving!) so the journeys add to the specialness of my Sundays by giving me a little relief. We don't talk much in the car. Angus's mind is no doubt on the services, and I try to do what, I imagine, God did on the very first Sabbath of all, I look around at the beauty of his creation and absorb something of the wonder of it. The road between our churches could hardly be more beautiful as it winds its way down the Kintyre peninsula with the western fringes of the Atlantic Ocean lapping the shore in good weather and thrashing against the rocks in a most spectacular fashion when it's stormy. Sunday lunch is made on Saturday and heated in a microwave oven in the Campbeltown church hall in order that I don't have to spend the precious little while at home on Sunday afternoons cooking a meal. I spend it sleeping instead! If I didn't, I'd not have the energy or mental alertness to benefit from the evening service, the only one that I'm able to sit right through. Perhaps when we retire it will be different, but if it is, I hope there will still be time to enjoy the beauty of God's creation every Sabbath as well as to celebrate the resurrection of the Living Lord.

Keeping the first part of the Sabbath commandment is, in a way, easy compared to keeping the second. That can be as fraught today as it was when Jesus seemed to be in constant trouble over it. We can control what happens in our own homes, but what about our influence on society? How can we use this commandment as a tool in the communities in which we live? I imagine most Christians avoid shopping on Sundays other than in real emergencies, but we read Monday's newspapers that are produced on Sundays and put mail in the post on Saturday expecting it to arrive on Monday! Do we really think it lies still somewhere all of Sunday? But before we get ourselves into the same knot that the Pharisees, we should remind ourselves of what Jesus said on the subject. 'The Sabbath was made for man, not man for the Sabbath. So the Son of Man is Lord even of the Sabbath.' It is our job to work out for ourselves the most God-glorifying way in which we can keep the fourth Commandment, remembering that it is given to us as a rule to keep and a tool to use for our refreshment and re-creation, and for the benefit of society too.

16

The

HONOURING PARENTS

TOOLBAR

God says, 'Honour your father and your mother, so that you may live long in the land the Lord your God is giving you' (Exod. 20: 12). The first three Commandments focus on the Lord and our relationship with him. The fourth bridges the gap between that and our relationships with other people, in that we keep the Sabbath day holy because it is a Sabbath to the Lord our God, but it also involves being responsible for others. With the fifth Commandment we move on to how we live and relate to those among whom we share our lives right from earliest childhood.

Parenthood is part of God's order of creation, and in some way or another every variety of living thing becomes the parent of something yet to come. On one of my morning walks a few weeks ago the Lord opened my eyes to see his provision for next year. I was standing beneath a sycamore tree that had appeared, from the distance, just a little bit odd. But when I stood underneath it and looked up I realised that the hundreds of little dark clusters hanging from it were embryonic sycamore seeds growing inside their own personal helicopters! That made me look around and I realised that although it was just springtime the Lord had already prepared for new seeds sprouting in spring of next year. The rowan flowers were fading and its tiny green berries were just beginning to appear, bluebells were setting seed and early dandelion parachutes already floated in the air. Like a child, I picked a dandelion clock and blew the seeds to the wind for the sheer joy of it! A few days later I read part of Genesis 1 to my Sunday School class. 'Then God said, "Let the land produce vegetation: seed-bearing plants and trees ..."' (v. 11). 'What would have happened if God had made plants and trees that were not seed-bearing?' I asked. Being country children they knew the answer right away. 'Everything would have died out at the end of the first generation,' I was told.

So much depends on God's gift of parenthood: the future of all that lives on our planet and the future of mankind himself. God's rule is clear enough: Honour your father and mother. Although tainted by sin since before their birth, most young children do to a greater or lesser degree honour their parents, or whoever is bringing them up. They are their authority figures, teachers, providers, carers, playmates and friends. I never really thought of our children honouring us until they started school and began to question what they had previously accepted. And where there were differences between home and school, we began to hear, 'But my teacher says ...' I wonder if other parents remember that as clearly as I do; it seemed to mark the beginning of a new era in family life.

The Bible provides us with some tools which help teach us how to honour our parents, whether they are young or in later years, and how to help our children to honour us. 'Children, obey your parents in the Lord, for this is right'

(Eph. 6:1). That, however, is followed by a word to fathers. 'Do not exasperate your children; instead, bring them up in the training and instruction of the Lord' (v. 4). Honour is insisted upon, but Christian parents help their children to honour them when they are reasonable in their behaviour and when they try to bring their young up according to God's rules. The writer of Proverbs was able to say, 'Listen, my son, to your father's instruction and do not forsake your mother's teaching' (Prov. 1:8), because their teaching was based on God's Word. What was being taught – by example as well as word – was geared towards the child's spiritual growth and development. 'My son, if you accept my words and store up my commands within you ... then you will understand the fear of the Lord and find the knowledge of God' (Prov. 2:1, 5). Children brought up in Christian homes should find good reason for honouring their parents, poor frail creatures though they be, and in doing so they are honouring the Lord through his gift of family life and nurturing.

When children dishonour their parents, especially when the social structure encourages such behaviour, God's judgement is never far away. Think of Europe in the sixteenth and seventeenth centuries, where children of Bible-believing parents were used to try to influence them towards idolatry. Think of Communist China in the 1950s and 60s, where children were taught to spy on their parents and inform the authorities of 'deviant' behaviour. And think of today in Britain and America where children are encouraged to laugh at the very thought that God might have created all things as described in the Bible, even if that is what they are taught at home by their Christian parents. The honouring of parents is one of God's ten fundamental rules for the smooth running of society, however warped and damaged by the Fall, whether the parents are believers or not, and we really do ignore it at our peril.

Honour involves love, respect, obedience, concern and sometimes, especially in later years, provision. It involves loving even when that is difficult, respect even when we have to look hard to find reasons for it, obedience within the constraints of right and wrong, and concern for their good. As the years pass relationships change, and many adult sons and daughters find themselves almost in a situation of role-reversal, where their parents begin to become dependent on them rather than the other way round. Jesus was approached by some who were in that very position, but they were trying to squirm out of their responsibilities by claiming that their religious duties took precedence over their duty to their parents. The Lord would have none of it.

'So the Pharisees and teachers of the law asked Jesus, "Why don't your disciples live according to the tradition of the elders ..." And he said to them: "You have a fine way of setting aside the commands of God in order to observe your own traditions! For Moses said, 'Honour your father and mother,' and, 'Anyone who curses his father or mother must be put to death.' But you say that if a man says to his father or mother: 'Whatever help you might otherwise have received from me is Corban' (that is, a gift devoted to God), then you no longer let him do anything for his father and mother. Thus you nullify the word of God by your tradition that you have handed down. And you do many things like that"' (Mark 7:5, 9-13). How dare they use religion to try to get out of their God-given duty!

In my mother's latter years she began to lose her short-term memory and become a little confused. Because she lived alone, my father having died many years before, the family took a little while to realise what was happening. Small things gave us clues, though some of them left me more confused than I suspect she was! One morning, when she was on a visit to our home, she had a long lie. By the time she arose I had been into town for the shopping and the newspaper. 'What day is it?' Mum asked, when she came into the sitting room. 'Wednesday,' I answered. 'No, it's not,' she said. 'It's Tuesday.' There being nothing to be gained from arguing, I dropped the matter and handed her the newspaper to read with her cup of tea. She looked at it then commented, 'That's tomorrow's paper.' To this day I don't know if she was muddled – or just much smarter than me!

Just a few months before she died, Mum spent some time with us. I was writing a book and at the stage of checking the manuscript for mistakes. She knew she was losing her memory and was delighted when that could be put to good use. Having been an avid reader all of her life, Mum was a splendid proof-reader. Her memory loss meant that she could read a manuscript, making corrections as she went along and then start at the beginning again right away – having already forgotten what she'd read – and see more corrections that needed to be made. Most people, me included, rarely see mistakes missed on first reading because they read what they think is there rather than what is actually there. It gave Mum a great thrill to use her memory loss to advantage.

I know that it is not always easy to honour our parents, and I acknowledge that my mother made it easy for me. I'm also aware that had my father lived to old age things might have been very different. But God has laid it on the line, and there is no way around it. Interestingly, this command comes with a promise. 'Honour your father and your mother, so that you may live long in the land the Lord your God is giving you.' Blessings follow from the keeping of God's Law, and that would seem to be especially the case with the fifth Commandment.

17

TOOLS NOT WEAPONS

God says, 'You shall not murder' (Exod. 20:13). Jesus enlarges on the Commandment. He says, 'You have heard that it was said to the people long ago, "Do not murder, and anyone who murders will be subject to judgment." But I tell you that anyone who is angry with his brother will be subject to judgment. Again, anyone who says to his brother, "Raca," is answerable to the Sanhedrin. But anyone who says, "You fool!" will be in danger of the fire of hell. Therefore, if you are offering your gift at the altar and there remember that your brother has something against you, leave the gift there in front of the altar. First go and be reconciled to your brother; then come and offer your gift' (Matt. 5:21-24). The word 'raca' means empty, worthless, and seems to have been, in Jesus' day, a little less insulting than calling someone a fool, which was a very damning insult indeed.

When we take the Commandment and place it alongside Jesus' enlargement, its seriousness becomes evident. Most of us can look at the sixth commandment and feel virtuous in the knowledge that we've never murdered anyone. But that virtue drains when we discover that the desire to hurt and insult is, in the eyes of our righteous God, tantamount to the act of murder itself. So serious is it, says Jesus, that if we are brewing ill-feeling for someone, we must sort it out before we should even think of attending public worship! God does not take ill-feeling lightly.

Many years ago I was hurt by someone in an accident that, like many 'accidents', might have been avoided. I don't think I felt a great deal of ill-will for him, though I might be quite wrong, and the friend who gave me the following advice may have known me better than I knew myself. My friend told me that you can't sincerely pray for someone's good and hate him at the same time. He was right; prayer is the most powerful tool against ill-will.

John Wesley wrote:

> Do all the good you can,
> By all the means you can,
> In all the ways you can,
> In all the places you can,
> At all the times you can,
> To all the people you can,
> As long as ever you can.

Perhaps he was paraphrasing the Lord's words. 'In everything, do to others what you would have them do to you ...' (Matt. 7:12). Interestingly, the Lord concludes that sentence with, '... for this sums up the Law and the Prophets.' That includes the sixth Commandment.

The most effective means of disarming your enemy, it has often been said, is to make him your friend. How true that is. But how do we go about that? What are the tools available to us for befriending those who have hurt us in whatever way? First among them is prayer. My friend was absolutely right about that. I think that next on the list is the honest realisation that nearly every time there is a rift in a relationship there are two sides to the story, even if we don't know them both.

Scripture gives an account of a 'sharp disagreement' in the Book of Acts. Paul approached Barnabas with the suggestion that they revisit the towns in which they had preached to see how the young churches were getting on. Barnabas agreed and wanted to take John Mark along with them. But Paul, who remembered that the last time the young man was with them he had not stayed the course, strongly opposed the idea. The two church leaders, Barnabas and Paul 'had such a sharp disagreement that they parted company'. Barnabas, taking John Mark with him, left for Cyprus to preach the gospel there. And Paul, who chose the more reliable Silas for a companion, went to Syria and Cilicia (from Acts 15:36-41).

No doubt Paul felt that John Mark had had his chance, that the cause of the gospel should not be held back by a young man's lack of stickability. Barnabas, the encourager, took a different view, probably seeing the potential that was there to be nurtured in John Mark, the potential that saw its eventual fulfilment in the gospel the young man wrote. Perhaps he was better at writing than at being a travelling evangelist. Years later, when Paul wrote to Timothy from Rome, among his instructions was, 'Get Mark and bring him with you, because he is helpful to me in my ministry' (2 Tim. 4:11). We don't know how it happened, but Paul and Mark seem to have been friends in the end.

Why is that story in the Book of Acts? I think one reason God placed it in the canon of Scripture is to remind us that Christians are not above falling out with one another. In fact, we do it so often on 'points of principle' that over the centuries the church could be said to have multiplied by division. That is not to our credit. The story also adds credence to the authenticity of Scripture. If well-meaning Christians had edited the Book of Acts, other than under the guidance of God, they might have air-brushed out the 'little incident' that reflected sadly on the heroes of the faith.

Praying for those with whom we are in disagreement and trying to see that there are two sides to every row – even between believers – is just the beginning of putting things right again. Christ's 'do to others as you would have them do to you' is the practical way forward. Any serious rift should set us thinking, and perhaps our thinking might be along these lines.

- An admission – I feel I'm in the right, but I must still have contributed something to the current impasse.
- A fact – repeating my point of view in ever increasing decibels is only going to inflame the situation.
- A question – does it matter? Is the point over which we are arguing worth what it is doing to us? Really?
- A move – am I willing to make the first move, because that's what I'd really like him to do? (Do to others as you would have them do to you – remember?)
- A humble apology – ditto.
- An act of kindness – apologies cemented by acts of kindness help hurts to heal.

'"In your anger do not sin." Do not let the sun go down while you are still angry, and do not give the devil a foothold'

(Eph. 4:26-27). Speed is implied in Jesus' explanation of the sixth Commandment as those who were at odds with each other were not to attend public worship until they had resolved their problem. Serious disagreements do not improve with keeping. Robert Burns, the Scottish poet, wrote of a wife waiting for her drunken husband to come home at night. As she waited she was 'nursing her wrath to keep it warm'. And I don't think that there is a single one of us who doesn't know exactly what that feels like.

18

TOOLS THAT ENCOURAGE FAITHFULNESS

God says, 'You shall not commit adultery' (Exod. 20:14). Jesus expands on the theme. 'You have heard that it was said, "Do not commit adultery." But I tell you that anyone who looks at a woman lustfully has already committed adultery with her in his heart' (Matt. 5:27-28). Just as murder, actual or wishful, is an outrage against God's gift of life, so adultery, actual or wishful, is an outrage against his gift of marriage. Having made Eve as a 'suitable helper' for Adam, our first father recognised her for what she was intended to be. 'This is now bone of my bones and flesh of my flesh; she shall be called "woman", for she was taken out of man.' And God's Word adds the conclusion, 'For this reason a man will leave his father and mother and be united to his wife, and they will become one flesh. The man and his wife were both naked, and they felt no shame' (Gen. 2:21-25).

Right from the institution of marriage the relationship was intended to be exclusive. The two became one. They were no longer two people, they were one couple – and they should stay that way. Jesus said, '… at the beginning of creation God "made them male and female". "For this reason a man will leave his father and mother and be united to his wife, and the two will become one flesh." So they are no longer two, but one. Therefore what God has joined together, let man not separate' (Mark 10:6-9). Marriage is the building block of society as God intended it to be. Only those who are trying to undermine society have made serious efforts to destroy marriage and the family, which makes current political thinking very sinister indeed.

When Angus and I had been married for just a few years a young woman visited me. She was engaged to be married and both she and her fiancé were Christians. Her parting comment, that really took my breath away, was this: 'It's a comfort to know that if it doesn't work out we can always get a divorce.' I'm glad to say that they are still married some thirty years later. Before that – it would be about 1975 – I don't think I'd ever heard of a Christian couple divorcing, and I'd certainly never come across a believer who went into marriage reassured because divorce was there as an escape route. In a way I am surprised that the couple are still together as it is my experience that if you go into something with an eye on the exit, you usually end up going through it sooner rather than later.

A young couple, newly married and with eyes only for each other, would surely agree with Thomas à Kempis – though they might want to update his language. 'Nothing is sweeter than love, nothing more courageous, nothing higher, nothing wider, nothing more pleasant, nothing fuller nor better in heaven and earth; because love is born of God, and cannot rest but in God, above all created things. He that loveth flies with wings, runneth and rejoiceth because he is free and not bound. Love feels no burdens, thinks nothing of trouble, attempts what is above all strength, pleads no excuse of impossibility; for it thinks all things lawful for itself and all things possible. It is therefore able to undertake all things, and it completes many things and brings them to a conclusion, where he who does not love faints and lies down.'

Marriage is liberating; it is the final freedom from parental control, yet how often we hear of couples who no longer want to 'be tied down' to each other. Marriage is sweet, the fullest earthly expression of love between two people, yet how many couples say their relationship has turned sour. Marriage is enabling, yet it is so often called restricting. Marriage is empowering, but couples sometimes drain each other until there is no love left. What is it that takes a dewy-eyed couple and makes them querulous, that changes a happy home into a battleground? As believers we need to ask these questions very seriously for there are Satanic forces working for the destruction of Christian marriage. The devil knows, even if we don't admit it, that in attacking the institution of marriage he is fighting to win a major victory.

We sometimes say that young couples in love only have eyes for each other. It sounds so sentimental, doesn't it? Well, sentimental it may sound, but I believe with all my heart that that is what keeps a couple together. As soon as eyes begin to wander Satan will provide attractive alternatives to be admired. That may go on for a while, each tempting thought being just a little more tantalising than the last one. But when eyes have become accustomed to wandering the devil is well able to turn admiration into lust, which is wishful adultery. Having let the marriage relationship slip to that degree, I guess that it takes a very strong husband or wife indeed to prevent adultery becoming actual rather than wishful. And even if it doesn't, the damage is done.

God made the rule foundational – you shall not commit adultery. What tools can we use to keep our marriages intact and loving, to still have eyes only for each other after long years of married life?

Prayer. It may be an old-fashioned comment, but there is much truth in it – couples who pray together, stay together. Praying with our marriage partner keeps our focus on the Lord. There should never be a day in a Christian marriage when a couple don't approach God's throne together, even if they have had a disagreement. And when they are separated they bear each other to the Lord in prayer.

Thanksgiving. Love and marriage are among God's most precious gifts. Making a daily practice of thanking the Lord for our marriage partner may help us to remember the preciousness of what we have been given. It is so easy to take people for granted. When Angus was ill for some months at the beginning of last year it looked for a time as though the problem might be very serious indeed. It turned out not to be. I can't describe the rush of thanksgiving that overcame me when I realised that God was going to allow us to enjoy his good gift of marriage for a little while longer, and then the conviction I felt when I had to admit that I didn't always feel so thankful because so often I take my husband for granted.

Nurturing love. Several of my friends are keen gardeners or have collections of house plants. For some years I kept a greenhouse and really enjoyed that. There is something about nurturing plants that is very satisfying. You watch the temperature of the water you give them, weed round about them to provide space to grow, feed them when they need a little nourishment and put them where they can be seen to their best advantage. The whole business of nurturing is satisfying for the person who does the nurturing, and it certainly does the garden or greenhouse a whole lot of good. It does marriage good too. How lovely it is to see a couple doing little things for each other, inconsequential things that mean so much. We had a couple in our congregation, in their eighties, who have now both died. When they went down the village they walked hand in hand as they had, I'm quite sure, sixty years before. I've no doubt they enjoyed that closeness, and many other people in the village seeing them did too. One of the things I really miss because I use crutches is walking hand-in-hand. Of another couple I knew I heard it said, 'They are always looking out for each other.' What a tribute to a marriage and what a challenge.

Be honest. It is so easy to let little troubles become big grudges just by keeping them, feeding them and letting them grow. How much better to settle accounts when the bill comes in, to sort out things as they happen. Better to have a discussion (even an argument?) at dinnertime than to lie awake all night in a gloom that matches the darkness of the hour.

Don't let the children get between us. Even quite small children can be manipulative, they can play dad off against mum in quite expert ways and sow seeds of real problems for the future. By their teen years some have developed it into an art form. We've all seen it in other families and the sad truth is that it is easier to recognise at that distance than it is closer to home.

Have a life. When one of our daughters was in her teens she asked us what we found to talk about when she and her sisters were not there. The amazing assumption was that we had nothing in our lives apart from them! By necessity our children do take up much of our lives, most of our energy (at least that's what it feels like sometimes), and substantial tracts of our time. But we bring them up in order to send them out to have lives of their own, and we must be really careful to hold on to enough of our own life, and enough of each other, to still have a working and loving relationship when the children are up and off.

Share things. Some of the happiest couples I know are ones where they share some of their interests. They go hill-walking together, occasionally read the same book, watch the same film on television or listen to music together. Angus and I share an interest in family history. I suppose that will see us to the end of our days as the furthest back we have reached is the seventeenth century and there's a long way between there and Adam and Eve, even if you subscribe to the young earth theory! It is so easy to have quite different interests, therefore quite different sets of friends. Of course, believers have their Christian friends and congregational family in common and that is a great support structure for any marriage and family.

Guard the eyes. There will inevitably be times when we look up and find ourselves admiring some attractive person of the opposite sex. Perhaps that's when we should send an arrow prayer to heaven thanking the Lord for our husband or wife, and it is also when we should turn away and look at something else. In this day and age of over-exposed flesh, it can sometimes be a problem knowing where to look.

We have a promise-keeping God, and there is no better promise to cling to when thinking about marriage than this one. 'So, if you think you are standing firm, be careful that you don't fall! No temptation has seized you except what is common to man. And God is faithful; he will not let you be tempted beyond what you can bear. But when you are tempted, he will also provide a way out so that you can stand up under it' (1 Cor. 10:12-13).

19

Theft – and the tools of insight and contentment

God says, 'You shall not steal' (Exod. 20:15). We have never been burgled, but I know from others who have that it is a deeply disturbing experience. The thought of someone having gone through your drawers and wardrobes, touching your personal possessions and reading your diary and private papers is almost worse than having lost whatever was stolen. It's a violation of privacy, almost a rape of what belongs to you, quite apart from theft. We hold up our hands in horror at the thought that we are thieves when that's the kind of thing we think of as stealing.

Stealing has three different aspects: taking what does not belong to us, not returning what belongs to someone else, and not paying what we owe. I want to think about some of the ways in which we can be tempted into doing these things without, sometimes, even recognising we are breaking God's law. I hope that doing so will give us the insight, the tools, to begin to avoid such sin.

Taking what does not belong to us

All that we have belongs to the Lord. When we misuse our time, our money, our energy or our affection we steal from him. We are only stewards of what we 'possess' on earth. Even our children are given to us in trust for a time, and should we put obstacles in their rightful path towards independence for our own selfish reasons we steal from the Lord as well as committing an act of theft against them.

Praise due to God certainly does not belong to us, frail creatures that we are. Nothing massages our conceit more soothingly than praise. 'What a wonderful mother you are to have all your children converted.' 'You're an amazing preacher. People come to faith at every service.' 'Your books help me so much I read them over and over again.' 'Your prayers are beautiful. They take me right to the throne of grace.' 'The letter you wrote said just what God wanted me to know.' How easy it is to take sincere and well-meant thanks and translate it into praise and then to bask in it – having stolen it from the Lord God, through whom alone we are able to do or say any good.

We do not own other people's private lives and to spread intimate details – even if shared with us for the purpose of prayer – is theft. Christians are good at shaking our heads at the thought of gossip, then gossiping ourselves. Perhaps we call it a burden we feel we must pass on, or a very confidential prayer request. But if we are told something confidentially and then pass it on to other people, we commit an act of theft. We steal the trust and the privacy of the person who shared her heart.

Our decisions belong to us; other people's decisions belong to them and are their responsibility. God has given us a great gift in the Christian community, the gift of family life together. We are all children of our heavenly Father, therefore brothers and sisters through Christ. That does not mean we can run our sisters' lives or put undue pressure on our brothers to make choices as we see fit. Sadly in the Christian church there is a tendency to translate filial love into power and to disempower the weaker or less decisive members of our community. This is theft.

People's reputations belong to them, and to do anything to take away from their reputations is stealing. We all know how it is done. A quiet word that casts doubt on someone's judgment is all it takes; even a thoughtless comment can destroy a good reputation. And good reputations take years to build and just minutes to destroy. The late Archbishop Winning of Glasgow likened character assassination to murder. He was right. Even Christians sometimes cannot avoid hearing scandal, but we certainly can avoid passing it on. In fact, we should be so well-known for our disinterest in gossip and scandal that those who indulge in it do not pass it on to us.

Not returning what belongs to someone else

Why is it that those of us who would never dream of borrowing money and not returning it at the earliest possible opportunity, borrow books and DVDs and CDs quite freely and then 'put them away' among our own belongings, only to be surprised – and a little embarrassed – a very long time later. I wonder if we did that with a taped sermon on 'You shall not steal,' we'd have the courage to return it when we realised what we'd done!

Do we return thanks when it's due, or do we steal it in-stead? People do us good all of the time, a little note here, an encouraging word there, a pat on the arm in the passing, a hug when the pressure is on. It takes just a minute to return their goodness and say thank-you. The thoughtlessness that so often prevents us doing that is theft.

Do we return favours? Young mothers often organise themselves into baby-sitting circles. It's a splendid way of arranging child-care, especially in the Christian community. They usually run something like this – mums decide on how many 'tokens' they have, say they agree on six over the course of three months. They can then call on others to baby-sit six times, but they have to be prepared to return the favour on the same number of occasions. That's a fairly formal arrangement, but when people do us a favour do we look for a way of returning the favour or passing it on? I know someone who from time to time 'lends' small amounts of money to students. She explains that she doesn't want it back, but when they have qualified and are earning they should seek out impoverished students and return the favour. Do we return favours or steal the opportunity?

Not paying what we owe
God was displeased with his people in Malachi's day because they did not give him what they owed. They owed sacrifices of perfect animals, the rules for which were spelled out in the books of the Law. The Lord's message through his prophet was stern. "'When you bring injured, crippled or diseased animals and offer them as sacrifices, should I accept them from your hands?" says the Lord. "Cursed is the cheat who has an acceptable male in his flock and vows to give it, but then sacrifices a blemished animal to the Lord. For I am a great king," says the Lord Almighty, "and my name is to be feared among the nations'" (Mal. 1:13-14). Do we bring offerings to the Lord

according to how he has prospered us, or are we stealing from him by engaging in tokenism?

If we employ people and do not pay them promptly, we steal from them. God says, 'I will come near to you for judgment. I will be quick to testify against … those who defraud labourers of their wages …' (Mal. 3:5). Many small businesses fail, not because the work is sub-standard, but because accounts are not settled on time. Perhaps as Christians we should make it our priority to pay accounts immediately they come in. The old saying is that we should keep short accounts with God; we should also keep short accounts with those who do work for us, or with those people and companies who supply us with goods and services.

Theft's antidote

The antidote to theft is generosity, the love of giving rather than acquiring. Paul said, 'Now I commit you to God and to the word of his grace, which can build you up and give you an inheritance among all those who are sanctified. I have not coveted anyone's silver or gold or clothing. You yourselves know that these hands of mine have supplied my own needs and the needs of my companions. In everything I did, I showed you that by this kind of hard work we must help the weak, remembering the words the Lord Jesus himself said: "It is more blessed to give than to receive"' (Acts 20:32-35).

The blessing of giving is not confined to the wealthy and those who can afford to be generous. 'Jesus sat down opposite the place where the offerings were put and watched the crowd putting their money into the temple treasury. Many rich people threw in large amounts. But a poor widow came and put in two very small copper coins, worth only a fraction of a penny. Calling his disciples to him, Jesus said, "I tell you the truth, this poor widow has put more into the treasury than all the others. They all gave out of their wealth; but she, out of her poverty, put in everything – all that she had to live on'" (Mark 12:41-44).

The manner of our giving is important. Theft is devious and dark; generous giving is a joyous affair, though not an ostentatious one. God's Word says, 'Remember this: Whoever sows sparingly will also reap sparingly, and whoever sows generously will also reap generously. Each man should give what he has decided in his heart to give, not reluctantly or under compulsion, for God loves a cheerful giver' (2 Cor. 9:6-7).

20

TRUTH RULES AND TRUTH TOOLS

God says, 'You shall not give false testimony against your neighbour' (Exod. 20:16). The keeping of the ninth Commandment would, like the keeping of those that precede it, tend towards an orderly society. Even in the best ordered societies, however, there are disagreements and disputes that end up in the law courts. In his provision for that, God insists on truthful testimony. However astute judges are, cases rest on the veracity of the testimonies delivered. The Commandment specifically relates to 'your neighbour', a member of the household of God, though Jesus widens the term 'neighbour' to include all with whom we come in contact. When the Lord was asked the question, 'Who is my neighbour?' he answered with the story of the Good Samaritan, thus showing how widely he expected the word to be interpreted.

Another aspect of truthfulness in a legal context is to be found in Leviticus. 'If a person sins because he does not speak up when he hears a public charge to testify regarding something he has seen or learned about, he will be held responsible' (5:1). Not only is truth imperative in testifying when a witness is called to do so, witnesses are also legally responsible – in terms of God's law – for coming forward if they have seen (or even heard an account of) anything pertinent to a case. God's Word makes it clear that it is a sin to withhold evidence, even if that evidence is second-hand. For lack of evidence an innocent party might be found guilty or a guilty party acquitted. In the sight of God the wrong outcome would be held against the witness who did not come forward just as surely as if he had told a lie in court.

It is a sad fact that Jesus himself was the victim of false witnesses. 'The chief priests and the whole Sanhedrin were looking for false evidence against Jesus so that they could put him to death, but they did not find any. Many testified falsely against him, but their statements did not agree' (Mark 14:55-56). Unable to pin guilt on the Lord in that way, the Sanhedrin went on to listen to those who gave false interpretations of what Jesus had said about destroying the temple and rebuilding it in three days. But lest we think that Jesus' life was seized from him, we should remember that it was only when Christ himself admitted the charge that he was condemned. 'The high priest said to him, "I charge you under oath by the living God: Tell us if you are the Christ, the Son of God." "Yes, it is as you say," Jesus replied. ... "He is worthy of death," they answered' (Matt. 26:63-64, 66). The Lord's life was not seized from him; he laid it down as a ransom for his people.

God's Word warns about the danger of the uncontrolled tongue: '... the tongue is a small part of the body, but it makes great boasts. Consider what a great forest is set on fire by a small spark. The tongue also is a fire, a world of evil among the parts of the body. It corrupts the whole person, sets the whole course of his life on fire, and is itself set on fire by hell' (James 3:5-6). Boasts (v. 5) are lies by another name as they give a deliberately untrue impression. Slander is also lying, as it spreads falsehood. It is specifically condemned in the Bible. 'Do not go about spreading slander among your people' (Lev. 19:16). Jesus is the Truth, and truth is what he demands of those who are called by his name.

When I was a young Christian I was involved in beach missions for several years. Most team members were in their late teens and early twenties. It was not uncommon for mission leaders to say, among all the other advice they gave us, 'Remember who you are.' It was a timely reminder that we belonged to Jesus, we were bearing his name publicly, and we should be very careful what we did and what we said. That seems a good starting point in truth-keeping. Jesus said, 'I am the way and the truth and the life. No-one comes to the Father except through me' (John 14:6). He is the Truth. We are his blood-bought people and truth ought to be the hallmark of our lives. Lies are from Satan's territory. Jesus said to those who were determined to kill him, 'You belong to your father, the devil, and you want to carry out your father's desire. He was a murderer from the beginning, not holding to the truth, for there is no truth in him. When he lies, he speaks his native language, for he is a liar and the father of lies' (John 8:44).

Truth is part of the Christian's armour. 'Stand firm then, with the belt of truth buckled around your waist ...' (Eph. 6:14). An unarmed off-duty soldier is vulnerable, especially if he is in enemy territory and is recognised for who he is. We live in enemy territory, Satan has us marked, and he is no doubt delighted when we take time off from the Lord's service and remove our armour and relax. And he's right in there with all guns of temptation blazing. Christians are never off-duty. We are soldiers of the Lord from the very day he becomes our Master until the day he releases us from service here on earth and takes us home to heaven. Being ever conscious of that should help us in our truth-keeping.

A friend of mine passed on this advice from her childhood. When you are tempted to tell a lie, touch your belt – or where a belt would be if you were wearing one – to remind you that the belt of God's truth is buckled around your waist. Do it every time you are tempted to tell a lie, every time you want to exaggerate (add so much to the truth that it becomes a lie) and every time you want to boast. Simple things like that remind us to watch our conversation, to be careful what we say, to remember who we are. And simple things do work!

It is so easy to slip into lying without even realising that what we are saying is not true. Our daffodils remind me of that. When we moved to our present home I bought a bag of daffodil bulbs that were planted in the back garden. They have been a source of delight every year since. Normally daffodils boom here between March and May, but these ones started blooming on 27th February after they were planted. The following year it was 18th January. In 2000 they bloomed on 7th January and again on 21st December. In 2001 the first one was out on 24th November. The earliest they have ever bloomed was in 2004, when we were amazed to find the first daffodil on 12th November! No wonder they give us such pleasure. During a talk I gave at a ladies' meeting, I mentioned how much I enjoyed looking at them from my study window. A friend listened to a tape of the talk and enquired if I'd been using artist's licence. When I asked what she meant, Sandra reminded me that I can't see the daffodils from my study window at all. In fact, I have to climb the steps up to our back garden to see them. In a way I do see these lovely flowers as I look out the window as they 'flash upon the inward eye', as Wordsworth said about his daffodils. But the truth is that I told a lie that is perpetuated any time someone listens to the tape. It is just so easy to do.

Soon after that we had a dear missionary lady staying with us for a few days while I edited a book she had written. As she read through the manuscript and considered each suggested correction, her whole concern was to ensure that the truth was told, that there was not so much as a suggestion of a lie in the account of her life. She was an example and a lesson to me. She took God's Word very seriously indeed. 'The Lord detests lying lips, but he delights in men who are truthful' (Prov. 12:22). 'You were taught, with regard to your former way of life, to put off your old self, which is being corrupted by its deceitful desires; to be made new in the attitude of your minds; and to put on the new self, created to be like God in true righteousness and holiness. Therefore each of you must put off falsehood and speak truthfully to his neighbour, for we are all members of one body' (Eph. 4:22-25).

21

THE ANTI-COVETING TOOLBAR

God says, 'You shall not covet your neighbour's house. You shall not covet your neighbour's wife, or his manservant or maidservant, his ox or donkey, or anything that belongs to your neighbour' (Exod. 20:17). At the time at which the Lord gave the Law through Moses people lived much more simply than we do now. They replaced things when they were irreparably broken rather than when they were tired of them. Unless they were very wealthy, people didn't have more possessions than they needed. The same was true when Jesus was on earth. He knew the dos and don'ts of repairing wineskins and patching clothes. But it seems that even in a truly make-do-and-mend society there was still the temptation to be covetous, to want what someone else had, whether person, animal or object.

When I was a child it was no shame to go to school with a darn on the elbow of a jersey or a patch on the upper of a leather shoe. By the time I was teaching, just a few years later, a child would have forged an absence note rather than do that. The discussion in the playground was beginning to be about wearing the 'right' thing, though labels were still worn out of sight or cut off to prevent them scratching! It took another twenty years for the 'right' thing to become the designer label, and for labels to be worn on the outside of garments. Now quite small children are dressed in designer clothes – and know it. If ever there was encouragement to covet, that is it.

Why does God legislate against coveting? Scripture tells us that 'Godliness with contentment is great gain. For we brought nothing into the world, and we can take nothing out of it. But if we have food and clothing, we will be content with that. People who want to get rich fall into temptation and a trap and into many foolish and harmful desires that plunge men into ruin and destruction. For the love of money is a root of all kinds of evil. Some people, eager for money, have wandered from the faith and pierced themselves with many griefs' (1 Tim. 6:6-10). There is progression in these verses. If we have what we need we should be content with that. Discontentment comes when we want more than we have, riches of whatever kind. That's a trap, says God's Word, that encourages foolish and harmful desires and its end is destruction. Note what happens next, Scripture moves from having 'things' to wanting money and from wanting money to loving it. It is a real downward spiral, and the awful thing about it is that believers are caught up in it. No wonder they were pierced with many griefs.

Covetousness and contentment are exact opposites. Those who are covetous are discontented and those who are content do not covet. It would seem, therefore, that the tool to be used in the keeping of the tenth Commandment is the tool of contentment. Paul had learned a lesson on that subject. 'I know what it is to be in need, and I know what it is to have plenty. I have learned the secret of being content in any and every situation, whether well fed or hungry, whether living in plenty or in want' (Phil. 4:12). Paul's contentment was not dependent on having all that he wanted; sometimes he didn't even have what he needed. He had even known times of hunger. His was a contentment of the heart that rested on Christ in whom we have the greatest treasure of all.

Another tool that tends towards contentment and against covetousness is minding our own business. In order to want something belonging to our neighbour we need to know what our neighbour has. Only an ungodly interest in other people's possessions gives us a desire to own them ourselves. That doesn't mean that we should avoid visiting people in order not to see their new kitchen, or that we should refuse a lift home rather than enjoy the leather interior of our friend's new car. Rather we have to learn to rejoice with those who rejoice and be content with what we have been given.

When our children were young some friends and I discussed our family lives. One, who like me had been a teacher, had gone back to work. Her mother-in-law looked after her two little boys and loved it – so did they! Chris needed a car to travel to work as the school in which she taught was some way from home. Travelling meant she was not home until very near dinner time. As she didn't want to trouble her mother-in-law by asking her to cook, she bought a microwave oven, a freezer and a dishwasher. There were some covetous conversations then! It was years later that Chris told me that she would have liked to have given up work and looked after the boys until they went to school, but she couldn't. She had to continue working to pay for the long list of things she had bought in order to work!

My grandmother was one of the most contented people I ever knew, though she was in a wheelchair for the last years of her life and died when she was only sixty-three years old. She did not have an easy life. Her husband committed suicide soon after the First World War, having suffered appallingly from shellshock, no doubt worsened by the death of one of their four children a few months earlier. Granny worked as a laundry-maid to bring up her three remaining children. She must have felt great relief when all three married and established homes of their own. I'm glad to say that my grandmother had a happy second marriage, but sadness was never far away. Her son's wife died while he was serving in the Second World War, and one of her two daughters died totally unexpectedly leaving two little boys, aged just three and five. Yet Granny had a spirit of contentment. She was financially poor all her days, but she was rich in what mattered. When I look around my home and family I realise how blessed I am compared with her in terms of worldly comforts, but I wonder how much I share of her godly contentment.

Perhaps counting our blessings and rejoicing in what we have – including our wonderful Saviour – is another useful tool to use when tempted to covet. 'Rejoice in the Lord always. I will say it again: Rejoice! Let your gentleness be evident to all. The Lord is near. Do not be anxious about anything, but in everything, by prayer and petition, with thanksgiving, present your requests to God. And the peace of God, which transcends all understanding, will guard your hearts and minds in Christ Jesus' (Phil. 4:4-7). Our hearts and minds need to be guarded in our increasingly materialistic world in order that we know contentment rather than covetousness and enjoy the peace that passes all understanding.

> He that is down needs fear no fall,
> He that is low, no pride;
> He that is humble ever shall
> Have God to be his guide.
>
> I am content with what I have,
> Little be it or much;
> And, Lord, contentment still I crave
> Because thou savest such.
>
> Fullness to such a burden is
> That go on pilgrimage;
> Here little, and hereafter bliss,
> Is best from age to age.
>   (John Bunyan)

22

Help

When I began using a computer it reassured me to find a Help function on screen. There were, however, times in the early days when reading the help I was given was like swimming through mud as it seemed to uncover layer after layer of complication rather than enlightenment. It took time to realise that I was still trying to understand why my computer did what it did rather than learning to use it. Now the Help function is both reassuring and helpful! It was as though I had a problem with the car, called out the RAC and then tried to understand the engineer's explanation of what the problem was rather than thanking him for his help and advice, turning on the ignition and driving away. People like me are our own worst enemy!

We all struggle between needing help and the need to be independent. The toddler needs help to learn to walk and then, as soon as she finds her feet, she needs independence to be off exploring. The teenager needs financial help (over and over again!) and then needs the independence to spend it how he likes. The elderly couple need assistance to continue living in their own home but need independence to make their own decisions. The old lady in a nursing home needs help to eat her meal, but still needs the independence to insist that she does *not* like smoked fish. Our whole lives are spent swinging between our need for help and our need to retain independence. And that goes back a very long way. Was Adam and Eve's rebellion not a demand for independence? God said 'no,' but I'll make up my own mind. I'll live my life my way. Unholy independence found its first expression in the Garden of Eden and its voice has been heard ever since. It sometimes takes dire circumstances before we call out for help to the One who is always ready to hear and answer.

When Isobel Kuhn discovered that her boyfriend was also seeing another girl, she went to bed in despair. In *By Searching*, she describes what she was going through. 'Why go on with life? It has no purpose, only suffering. This would be a good time to slip out. There is that bottle in the bathroom marked Poison. A good long drink and your troubles will be over. A good idea. The only sensible solution. I jumped out of bed and started for the bathroom. … My hand was on the door knob when a deep groan, thrice repeated, broke the silence of the dark. It was my father, moaning in his sleep in the next room. I was not afraid, for I recognised my father's tones, but I was startled into remembrance of him. I stood with my hand on the knob debating. If I committed suicide Daddy would think I had gone to Hell. … In agony I turned and sat down on the edge of my bed and faced the darkest moment of my life.' That night Isobel cried out to God. 'If you will prove to me that you are, and if you will give me peace, I will give you my whole life. I'll do anything you ask me to do, go where you send me, obey you all my days.' She lay down on her bed and the next thing she knew it was morning, and she had the peace that came from taking the first tentative steps towards the Lord.

Over half a century later a young Scotswoman was in the pits. An alcoholic since her teens, she was deeply depressed. One night she followed a woman she knew to a Stauros meeting, not knowing it was a gathering of Christians who had been addicted to alcohol. The man leading the meeting saw May Nicholson, filthy, smelling of drink, and her clothes covered in cigarette burns. He prayed, 'Lord, I pray for that wee woman you've brought in here tonight. We can all see that she's filthy by looking at the outside of her but you know how much more filthy her heart is. Touch her and clean her.' May described what happened next. 'He prayed for me and all I could do was cry because I thought I was so worthless that I wasn't worth a prayer. ... "Do you want to be saved?" the man asked, after he'd spoken to me for a minute or two. I was puzzled. "Saved from what?" He was so patient. "Do you believe in God?" he enquired. "Yes," I replied. "I can honestly say I believe in God. But God doesn't want anything to do with the likes of me." "God didn't send his son Jesus to die for good folk. He sent him to die for sinners. Are you a sinner?" the man asked. "I'm the worst there ever was," I said, then broke down and cried my heart out. Before I left that room I asked the Lord Jesus to come into my life. There were no flashing lights; nothing spectacular happened. I didn't know what was meant to happen anyway. But I knew that things were different' (from *Miracles from Mayhem*).

Isobel Kuhn and May Nicholson both reached the pits of despair before they called out to God for help. He answered them, saved them and used them to his glory. Isobel and her husband worked for many years as missionaries among the Lisu people in China. May founded Preshal Trust that serves one of the neediest areas of Glasgow. Preshal is Gaelic for *precious*, and the aim of the Trust is to show the people who come along that they are precious. Poverty as well as alcohol and drug abuse are rife in the part of the city in which Preshal works, yet there are many there who have come to know the joy of the Lord because when they were in dark despair they went to the Trust, learned about Jesus and called out to him for help.

Not only those who come to the Lord for the first time come to him with 'Help!' on their lips. Believers need his help on an on-going basis. King David's life was tough and the psalms record many of his cries for help from heaven. 'O Lord, do not forsake me; be not far from me, O my God. Come quickly to help me, O Lord my Saviour' (Ps. 38:21-22). 'In my distress I called to the Lord; I cried to my God for help. From his temple he heard my voice; my cry came before him, into his ears' (Ps. 18:6). David came to the Lord in time of need in answer to God's invitation. Not only computers have a help function advertising their willingness to be of use. 'The Mighty One, God, the Lord, speaks and summons the earth from the rising of the sun to the place where it sets ... call upon me in the day of trouble; I will deliver you, and you will honour me' (Ps. 50:1, 15). What an encouragement it is to know that when we call out to God for help, when he delivers us for the first or the numberless time, *He* is honoured.

The Lord helps his people willingly. Jesus said, 'Come to me, all you who are weary and burdened, and I will give you rest. Take my yoke upon you and learn from me, for I am gentle and humble in heart, and you will find rest for

your souls. For my yoke is easy and my burden is light'
(Matt. 11:28-30). We know what it's like to be weary and
burdened and it is no shame to come to the One who
has determined our road, to the one who has shaped our
burden, and ask for his help.

Child of my love, lean hard,
And let me feel the pressure of thy care,
I know thy burden; I shaped it,
Poised in mine own hand, and made no proportion
In its weight to thine unaided strength;
For even as I laid it on I said, '
'So shall I keep my child within the circling arms
Of mine own love.' Here lay it down, nor fear
To impose it on a shoulder which upholds
The government of worlds. Yet closer come,
Thou are not near enough; I would embrace thy care,
So I might feel my child reposing on my breast.
Thou lovest me? I know it. Doubt not, then,
But, loving me, lean hard.

(From *Streams in the Desert* by Charles Cowman)

God is not only willing but able to answer our cries for help.
'My help comes from the Lord, the Maker of heaven and
earth. He will not let your foot slip – he who watches over
you will not slumber; indeed, he who watches over Israel will
neither slumber nor sleep. The Lord watches over you – the
Lord is your shade at your right hand; the sun will not harm
you by day, nor the moon by night' (Ps. 121:2-6). The Lord
our God is omniscient – he knows everything, including
our need for help. He is omnipotent – his power can meet
our every need. He is omnipresent – wherever we are we are
not outside the scope of his help. And he is glorified in our
weakness for it shows up his wonderful strength.

We can be sure that the Lord can answer our cries for help, not only today, but for all time. 'The Lord will keep you from all harm – he will watch over your life; the Lord will watch over your coming and going both now and for evermore' (Ps. 121:7-8). And lest we think that his care is just for time, his Word assures us that it extends to his people through all eternity. 'Surely goodness and love will follow me all the days of my life, and I will dwell in the house of the Lord for ever' (Ps. 23:6). The thought of being with the Lord for ever and for ever makes me want to write the words 'for ever' in large print then scroll them down the computer screen before printing them until I run out of paper just for the joy of knowing that forever is a very, very long time.

Just yesterday we heard of the death of a dear Christian friend, an elderly lady who had served the Lord for many years here on earth. Annie was a real prayer warrior, waking up at five each morning to pray through the long list of people whom the Lord had laid on her heart. Missionaries all over the world knew that Annie was praying for them. She was also given a ministry of letter-writing and I've lost count of the number of wonderfully spiritual letters that came just when they were needed and helped me. I don't think I ever received a letter from her that didn't quote the verse, 'Hitherto hath the Lord helped us' (1 Sam. 7:12, kjv). That was her experience; that was her testimony. And yesterday, when my heart was sore at the thought of not seeing our dear friend again this side of eternity, it was comforting to know that the Lord helped her right to the end and that she is now gloriously joyful in his nearer presence forever and ever and ever.

Annie was a fine example of those whom the Lord helps, for she was herself a helper. Her home, The Tav, was open to people with all kinds of needs and there are those who can look back and point to The Tav as their place of rebirth, and a great many others for whom it was a place of solace. She wasn't wealthy, but Annie had love enough and time enough for everyone. Our friend was one of those people who listened to what you said so carefully that she knew what your concerns were next time you met because she had remembered them in prayer in the period in between. We'll miss Annie for herself, for she was a great character, but we also know that we have lost one of our most supportive pray-ers. And that's a sore miss.

Those who have been helped by the Lord are called into the ministry of helpfulness. 'Carry each other's burdens, and in this way you will fulfil the law of Christ' (Gal. 6:2). Lest any of us begin to be tempted to feel proud of our helpfulness, the next verse goes on, 'If anyone thinks he is something when he is nothing, he deceives himself.' It is interesting to note how God prepares people to help others. Isobel Kuhn was deeply shaken as a student when a professor she admired cast doubts in her mind regarding the existence of God. Years later the Lord called her to minister to people who feared evil spirits rather than believed in God. From her own experience of doubting the existence of God she was able to reach out to others who doubted him too. May Nicholson, whose background was marked by poverty and alcohol abuse, has been led by the Lord to work with those who live in Glasgow's Govan, where poverty and alcohol abuse is endemic. When newcomers come into Preshal they are very often surprised to discover that the woman 'in charge' knows exactly what they are going through, because she has gone through it herself.

Christ told his followers about the final judgment, explaining that in that great day there will be two groups of people, one blessed by his Father and the other cursed and whose final destination is 'the eternal fire prepared for the devil and his angels'. His description of those who are blessed reads thus. 'For I was hungry and you gave me something to eat, I was thirsty and you gave me something to drink, I was a stranger and you invited me in, I needed clothes and you clothed me, I was sick and you looked after me, I was in prison and you came to visit me.' The Lord explained that 'the righteous' had no memory of seeing Jesus in all these situations of need and of ministering to him. In fact, they denied all knowledge of it. Jesus continued, 'The King will reply, "I tell you the truth, whatever you did for one of the least of these brothers of mine, you did for me."' The focus then turns to the cursed and they are told that they did not help Jesus when he was in need. Shocked, they insist that they never saw him in need. The implication is that, had they done so, they would have met his need. And the story ends with a damning (literally) indictment. 'I tell you the truth, whatever you did not do for one of the least of these, you did not do for me' (from Matt. 25:31-46).

Of course, if we saw Jesus in need we would rush to his help. But do we rush to help the hungry who are ever with us, the middle-aged man sitting on the pavement with his dog beside him? Or do we look in the other direction as we head to the shops to buy what we could possibly do well without? Do we help the stranger, or are we so taken in by our security-conscious age that we see strangers as suspicious rather than potential friends we've not yet met? How do we react when we meet someone whose clothes are dishevelled and none too clean? Do we give them a wide berth? And what about the sick? When we go into a hospital ward to visit someone we love, do we lower our gaze when we leave our friend's bed in order not to make eye-contact with anyone else in the ward? A smile costs nothing. And what about those in prison? Do we pray for them, far less visit them? It is just so easy to think that our little Christian world is the real world and forget what lies outside. Christ does not.

23

SHUT DOWN

At the end of my working day it gives me pleasure to tap the few keys that close down my computer for the night. There is a nice kind of finality about it. It makes a few rumblings then there is a satisfying silence; the day is done. For some that is how life ends, quickly and painlessly. That is how we all hope it will be for us.

When I was a child there were two words that I don't think I ever heard said, they were cancer and sex. Around the mid 1960s people began to use the expression 'the big C' for cancer, and by then I was at college and sex was talked about more easily there. Death, on the other hand, was talked about. It was part of family life. When my grandmother died I was nine years old and I was taken to see her body and 'to say goodbye'. The living room curtains were closed and remained so until after her funeral. Often the first we knew of a death in the area was when the curtains were drawn shut. There were rituals to be gone through and people knew what to do. Family, friends and neighbours fitted into these rituals. People knew when it was appropriate to visit a house in mourning; they knew to expect an invitation to see the remains. Close family stayed at home between the death and the funeral, a period of usually just two or three days. There was a quietness and a seemliness that has been all but lost, at least here in Britain.

Now a corpse is often removed to a 'chapel of rest' to await burial, or more often cremation. Sometimes a week or more elapses between death and a funeral. Family members, by necessity, return to work after two or three days and then take a day off for the funeral. Curtains remain open and there is nothing to mark out a house and family in mourning. When my brother died, the ten days between his death and funeral felt like some kind of limbo-land. Everything went on as normal, but nothing was normal at all. Things would never be quite the same again. There is something to be said for death rituals. If nothing else, they allow us to admit that a significant event has happened and that it affects us deeply.

Death is becoming increasingly sanitised; it is being turned into some kind of medical event which may, or may not, be totally final. How final is death when people are comforted because some of the organs belonging to the person they loved are now keeping someone else alive? I read of a woman who had lost her son in a road accident. She was quoted as saying that her son was still alive inside the person who had received his heart and that it was a great comfort to her that he had not 'really died' at all. The sharp edges of both birth and death are being air-brushed into a blur as medicine experiments with both ends of life. And we see this exemplified in the 'In memory' columns of our local newspapers where poems are written to the departed in such a way as makes it look as though they still read the personal notices in the hereafter!

But death is real. It is the wrenching apart of body and soul, and that is what it was meant to be. Death was never meant to be tidy or convenient. When we sanitise the end of life we are forgetting what it is all about. It is a curse. Adam and Eve were permitted to eat of every tree in the Garden of Eden – except one. When they ate the fruit of the tree of the knowledge of good and evil they brought the curse of God upon themselves. 'Cursed is the ground because of you; through painful toil you will eat of it all the days of your life. It will produce thorns and thistles for you, and you will eat the plants of the field. By the sweat of your brow you will eat your food until you return to the ground, since from it you were taken; for dust you are and to dust you will return' (Gen. 3:17-19). Death was not part of the order of creation; it is an intrusion, a disruption, a tearing into two parts what God made as one. It is awful.

Not only were Adam and Eve cursed in this appalling way, they were banished from the Garden of Eden, the beautiful place that had been their home. But there was mercy even in that. 'The Lord said ... "He must not be allowed to reach out his hand and take also from the tree of life and eat, and live for ever." So the Lord God banished him from the Garden of Eden to work the ground from which he had been taken. After he drove the man out, he placed on the east side of the Garden of Eden cherubim and a flaming sword flashing back and forth to guard the way back to the tree of life' (Gen. 3:22-24). Had Adam and Eve taken the fruit of the tree of life in their sinful state they would have condemned themselves and their descendants to an eternal life of sinfulness without hope of redemption. It was grace that drove them from Eden; it was grace that barred the way back.

Which brings us to another death, a death died in love. 'This is how God showed his love among us: He sent his one and only Son into the world that we might live through him. This is love: not that we love God, but that he loved us and sent his Son as an atoning sacrifice for our sins' (1 John 4:9-10). Eden's gate was sealed shut in order that heaven might be opened wide for all those for whom Christ died. It is Christ's death that changes death. Although it remains the last enemy to be overcome, for the believer it is also the gateway to heaven.

When a friend of ours was just completing his training for the ministry, we talked about the work he was about to do. 'What's your aim in the ministry?' someone asked. He thought for a minute then said, 'I think my aim is to teach people to die well; for if they are prepared to die well, they will live well.' I believe that to be profoundly true. But how can we live in order to prepare to die well? 'For you were once darkness, but now you are light in the Lord. Live as children of the light (for the fruit of the light consists in all goodness, righteousness and truth) and find out what pleases the Lord' (Eph. 5:8-10). God's children can search the scriptures to find out what pleases him and then pattern their lives on his pleasure. The very thought of being able to give God pleasure is almost too amazing to begin to take in, but that's what his Word says.

Jesus is the light of the world and Paul told the Ephesians – and us – to live as children of the light. Light energises and makes things grow. Over the years I have had many houseplants. Not all need direct sunlight, but they do all need light. Starved of light they weaken and become sickly. Instead of putting on a good show of leaves then flowers, they grow long and leggy in their effort to reach light. It takes light to make plants flower and fruit, and this verse tells us that those who live in the light of Jesus bear beautiful fruit: goodness, righteousness and truth.

In his letter to the Galatians, Paul gives a longer list of fruit: '… the fruit of the Spirit is love, joy, peace, patience, kindness, goodness, faithfulness, gentleness and self-control. … Since we live by the Spirit, let us keep in step with the Spirit' (Gal. 5:22-23, 25). And, knowing our proneness to sin, the Apostle adds, 'Let us not become conceited, provoking and envying each other' (v. 26). How well he knows the human heart. Imagine a small fellowship of believers, each trying to live by the Spirit. One recognises that he is beginning to bear the fruit of self-control – then loses it by becoming conceited! Another bears the fruit of kindness and a less mature member of the fellowship provokes him to see if his kindness is only skin deep. Yet another exhibits goodness and faithfulness to a degree that some in the fellowship find themselves envying their godly friend. Nobody said it would be easy!

Looking to others, no matter how far along the Christian way they have walked, will never inspire us as much as looking to the Lord himself. 'Therefore, since we are surrounded by such a great cloud of witnesses, let us throw off everything that hinders and the sin that so easily entangles, and let us run with perseverance the race marked out for us. Let us fix our eyes on Jesus, the author and perfecter of our faith, who for the joy set before him endured the cross, scorning its shame, and sat down at the right hand of the throne of God. Consider him who endured such opposition from sinful men, so that you will not grow weary and lose heart' (Heb. 12:1-3). What a wealth of practical instruction in just a few words!

As we try to live as well as we hope to die, we are indeed surrounded by a great cloud of witnesses, both on earth and in heaven. A long list of them is to be found in the previous chapter, going all the way back to Abel, son of Adam! They serve as *motivation* in the same way as a crowd watching a race. Then there is *elimination* – throwing aside the sin that entangles us. We are all different, prone to succumb to different temptations. It is our job to work out what tempts us and to throw it aside by avoiding the situations we find difficult, the people who influence us in the wrong direction, and thinking about the enjoyment of our besetting sins. *Participation* comes next, as we run the race. A race is effortful. You don't run races without realising you are doing so. Living as well as we hope to die is effortful, strenuous, and takes energy and stickability. It also takes *determination*. If we are not determined to reach the end we have never really begun.

The Christian life is a way to an end, not an end in itself. Any who try to live as believers without their eyes focused on heaven are not believers at all, but fine upstanding citizens of earth. And our *inspiration* is Jesus himself, on whom our eyes are fixed. It is in his strength that we live as we hope to die; he is the author and perfecter of our faith. The wonder of wonders is this, that the joy that was set before our beloved Saviour as he endured the cross was the joy of knowing that he was purchasing for himself a people. So when life is hard, when opposition comes from within and without, when failure rears its ugly head and we feel we've let the Lord down so often, too often, then, concludes the writer to the Hebrews, 'Consider him who endured such opposition from sinful men, so that you will not grow weary and lose heart.' And, having endured to the end, when our home-call comes we will fall asleep in Jesus.

24

RESTART

When I got a new PC a friend set it up for me, installing all the necessary programs. He then departed and left me to it. All went well for the whole afternoon. It did what I expected it to do and I was fairly comfortable with the new setup – until I tried to switch the brute off. Each time I shut it down the screen faded, the usual closing down rumblings took place in its internal organs and it switched itself off ... and on again. Several times I went through the routine, and the same thing always happened. I was beginning to think that there was a glitch in the system when I realised that my friend had set it at restart in order to complete installations and I'd not changed it back to shut down. Problem solved.

The restart command seems a good one with which to conclude this book because, for the Christian, there is no final shut down, just a restart at the beginning of life in all the glory of heaven. The metrical version of the twenty-third Psalm is very commonly chosen for Scottish funerals, with the last verse often the last thing sung before the end of the service.

Goodness and mercy all my life
shall surely follow me:
And in God's house for evermore
my dwelling place shall be.

I've heard it said that Goodness and Mercy are like the names of two sheepdogs in this Shepherd psalm. Like well-trained working dogs they follow the sheep, never lifting their eyes other than to look at their shepherd. When a sheep begins to stray they are right there to steer it back into the flock. When it lags behind, they chivvy it on. When it tires, the shepherd tells the dogs to slow the flock down and place the tired sheep in the centre in order to encourage it to go on. So guided through life by God's goodness and mercy we reach our eternal home at last.

Some things will not be in heaven, and I think that we'll be so caught up in the glory of Jesus that we won't miss them at all. In the revelation God gave him, John recorded words he heard spoken in heaven. 'Now the dwelling of God is with men, and he will live with them. They will be his people, and God himself will be with them and be their God. He will wipe every tear from their eyes. There will be no more death or mourning or crying or pain, for the old order of things has passed away' (Rev. 21:3-4). Imagine that! The truth is that we can't begin to imagine the wonder of life without the effects of the Fall because that is all we have ever known.

John was shown 'the Holy City, the new Jerusalem, coming down out of heaven from God, prepared as a bride beautifully dressed for her husband' (Rev. 21:2). We know our sinful selves well enough that we find it almost impossible to believe that the church will one day be the bride of Christ. Samuel Rutherford, the seventeenth century Scottish divine, wrote many letters from prison to his congregation in Anwoth, from whom he was separated by hundreds of miles because of the political situation at the time. In several of his letters he encouraged his people by reminding them that even the poor persecuted church of his day was part of the bride of Christ. 'Our love to him should begin on earth, as it shall be in heaven; for the bride taketh not, by a thousand decrees, so much delight in her wedding garment as she doth in her bridegroom; so we, in the life to come, howbeit clothed with glory as with a robe shall not be so much affected with the glory that goeth about us, as with the bridegroom's joyful face and presence.' Imagine! One day we shall see the Bridegroom's joyful face as, dressed in garments of his glorious righteousness, we are presented to him as his bride!

Two centuries later, Mrs Anne Ross Cousin, whose husband was a Free Church minister in the Scottish Borders, wrote a lengthy poem based on Samuel Rutherford's letters. It describes the ending of a life here on earth and its glorious entry to the eternal joys of heaven. With it I conclude this book and shut down my computer for the night.

The sands of time are sinking
The dawn of heaven breaks,
The summer morn I've sighed for
The fair sweet morn awakes.
Dark, dark has been the midnight,
But dayspring is at hand,
And glory-glory dwelleth
In Immanuel's land.

Oh! Well it is for ever
Oh! Well for evermore –

My nest hung in no forest
Of all this death-doomed shore:
Yea, let the vain world vanish,
As from the ship the strand,
While glory-glory dwelleth
In Immanuel's land.

There the Red Rose of Sharon
Unfolds its heartsome bloom
And fills the air of heaven
With ravishing perfume:
Oh! To behold its blossom,
While by its fragrance fann'd
Where glory-glory dwelleth
In Immanuel's land.

The King there in his beauty,
Without a veil is seen:
It were a well spent journey,
Though seven deaths lay between:
The Lamb, with his fair army,
Doth on Mount Zion stand,
And glory-glory dwelleth
In Immanuel's land.

Oh! Christ he is the fountain,
The deep sweet well of love!
The streams on earth I've tasted,
More deep I'll drink above:
There, to an ocean fulness,
His mercy doth expand,
And glory-glory dwelleth
In Immanuel's land.

Oft in yon sea-beat prison
My Lord and I held tryst,

For Anwoth was not heaven,
And preaching was not Christ;
And aye, my murkiest storm-cloud
Was by a rainbow spann'd,
Caught from the glory dwelling
In Immanuel's land.

But that he built a heaven
Of his surpassing love,
A little New Jerusalem,
Like to the one above,
'Lord take me o'er the water,'
Had been my loud demand,
Take me to love's own country,
Unto Immanuel's land.

But flow'rs need night's cool darkness,
The moonlight and the dew;
So Christ, from one who loved it,
His shining oft withdrew: –
And then, for cause of absence
My troubled soul I scann'd,
But glory shadeless, shineth
In Immanuel's land.

The little birds of Anwoth,
I used to count them blest, –
Now, beside happier altars
I go to build my nest:
O'er these there broods no silence,
No graves around them stand,
For glory, deathless, dwelleth
In Immanuel's land.

Fair Anwoth, by the Solway,
To me thou still art dear,

E'en from the verge of heaven,
I drop for thee a tear.
Oh! If one from Anwoth
Meet me at God's right hand,
My heaven will be two heavens,
In Immanuel's land.

I've wrestled on towards heaven
'Gainst storm, and wind and tide'
Now like a weary traveller
That leaneth on his Guide,
Amid the shades of evening,
While sinks life's lingering sand,
I hail the glory dawning
From Immanuel's land.

Deep waters cross'd life's pathway,
The hedge of thorns was sharp;
Now, these lie all behind me –
Oh! For a well tuned harp!
Oh! to join Hallelujah
With yon triumphant band,
Who sing, where glory dwelleth,
In Immanuel's land.

With mercy and with judgment
My web of time he wove,
And aye, the dews of sorrow
Were lustred with his love: –
I'll bless the hand that guided,
I'll bless the hand that plann'd
When throned where glory dwelleth
In Immanuel's land.

Soon shall the cup of glory
Wash down earth's bitt'rest woes,

Soon shall the desert briar
Break into Eden's rose;
The curse shall change to blessing –
The Name on earth that's bann'd
Be graven on white stone
In Immanuel's land.

Oh! I am my Beloved's,
And my Beloved's mine!
He brings a poor vile sinner
Into his 'house of wine':
I stand upon his merit,
I know no other stand,
Not e'en where glory dwelleth
In Immanuel's land.

I shall sleep sound in Jesus,
Fill'd with his likeness rise,
To love and to adore him,
To see him with these eyes: –
'Tween me and resurrection
But Paradise doth stand;
Then-then for glory dwelling
In Immanuel's land.

The bride eyes not her garment,
But her dear bridegroom's face,
I will not gaze at glory,
But on my King of Grace –
Not at the crown he giveth,
But on his pierced hand;
The Lamb is all the glory
Of Immanuel's land.

I have borne scorn and hatred,
I have borne wrong and shame,

Earth's proud ones have reproach'd me
For Christ's thrice-blessed name: –
Where God his seal set fairest
They've stampt their foulest brand,
But judgment shines like noonday
In Immanuel's land.

They've summoned me before them,
But there I may not come, –
My Lord says 'Come up hither',
My Lord says 'Welcome home!'
My kingly King, at his white throne,
My presence doth command,
Where glory-glory dwelleth
In Immanuel's land.

**Other books of interest
by
Irene Howat**

Stopped Work? Start Living!:

Encouraging stories of directions in new retirement

Irene Howat

Western society is undergoing a transformation. With more and more of us living into our eighties and nineties, elderly and retired people constitute a more significant sector of the population than ever before. For many, retirement is looked upon as an opportunity to take up residence at the golf club, however, for the Christian it can offer so much more!

With a wealth of experience and wisdom many Christians find retirement gives the opportunity to serve God in new and different ways. *Stopped Work? Start Living!* tells the story of retirees who, having left the workplace behind them, took up the challenge of further Christian service. These inspirational examples show us that whilst others may view retirement as a time to wind down, we as Christians should view it as a new opportunity to serve the Lord Jesus.

ISBN 978-1-84550-047-4

A Week in the Life of MAF:

Mission Aviation fellowship

Irene Howat

For five decades, Mission Aviation Fellowship (MAF) planes have been serving countless thousands of men, women and children, bringing medical care, emergency food, and Christian hope. In the places of deepest need they are serving as the air-arm of the church, enabling the work of aid and development agencies, missions, national churches and other local groups.

Using aircraft and electronic communication networks MAF overcomes barriers that isolate people from spiritual and physical help. These are remote places where flying is not a luxury but a lifeline. Operating over 130 aircraft from bases in 33 countries, today every three minutes, a MAF plane is taking off or landing somewhere in the world

Best selling author Irene Howat has compiled the accounts of MAF workers in the field and invites you to experience a week in their lives. Flying across deserts, jungles, mountains and swamps, be transported to some of the most inaccessible areas in the world with MAF employees who are giving hope to far-flung communities. From the Ecuadorian jungle to the wetlands of Bangladesh to the Mongolian plains prepare for take off on an exhilarating and eye opening journey that you will never forget.

ISBN 978-1-85792-940-9

Christian Focus Publications

publishes books for all ages

Our mission statement –

STAYING FAITHFUL

In dependence upon God we seek to help make His infallible Word, the Bible, relevant. Our aim is to ensure that the Lord Jesus Christ is presented as the only hope to obtain forgiveness of sin, live a useful life and look forward to heaven with Him.

REACHING OUT

Christ's last command requires us to reach out to our world with His gospel. We seek to help fulfill that by publishing books that point people towards Jesus and help them develop a Christ-like maturity. We aim to equip all levels of readers for life, work, ministry and mission.

Books in our adult range are published in three imprints.

Christian Focus contains popular works including biographies, commentaries, basic doctrine and Christian living. Our children's books are also published in this imprint.

Mentor focuses on books written at a level suitable for Bible College and seminary students, pastors, and other serious readers. The imprint includes commentaries, doctrinal studies, examination of current issues and church history.

Christian Heritage contains classic writings from the past.

Christian Focus Publications, Ltd
Geanies House, Fearn, Ross-shire,
IV20 1TW, Scotland, United Kingdom
info@christianfocus.com

For details of our titles visit us on our website
www.christianfocus.com